Hairy Pothead

The Stoned Sorcerer

A Potter Parody
By
L. Henry Dowell

BLACK BOX PUBLISHING

To my Muse –
Thank you for reminding me that magic
is real.

Chapter One

The Boy Who Smoked

His name, that is to say, the name his
mother gave him upon his birth, was not Hairy
Pothead. Let's be clear about that point right up
front. This was just what people; his relatives
in particular, had taken to calling him. For as
long as he could remember, which wasn't all
that far back...he had been that "hairy
pothead".

Perhaps his name had been something as
mundane as Ralph or Bill once upon a time,
but after years of hearing things like "Why
don't you get a life, ya' hairy pothead?" and
"When are you going to move out of my
basement, you hairy, good for nothing,
pothead?", the moniker had stuck. It was just
as well, for the name was an apt description.

Chapter One

His dark, brown hair was shaggy and always looked as if it needed a jolly good scrubbing. He also wore glasses that were thick, round and nerdy. The clothes he wore were always wrinkled and usually sported a mustard stain somewhere on them. As for the pothead part, well, that was accurate as well, in more ways than one. Firstly, he loved pot. He always had, as far back as he could recall, but truth be told, he HAD surrendered a brain cell or two to his favorite pastime. He'd tried other things of course. All of the popular designer stuff, guaranteed to alter one's mind and perception of the universe, but it always came back to pot. Weed. Grass. Mary Jane. His one true love.

There was another reason he was called Pothead though. A reason far more unusual and mysterious than one might expect, for you see, in the middle of his forehead was a scar shaped like a marijuana leaf.

Hairy had no earthly idea where the strange mark had come from, only that it had been considered "bitchin' cool" by the few friends he'd had growing up.

He lived in the basement of Number Five, Privet Drive, a house owned by his aunt and

The Boy Who Smoked

uncle, Dagwood and Blondie Doofus and their fatass, rapper wanna-be son, Dilbert Doofus. He had lived in their basement since he was a young man…well, younger than he was now, anyway. In fact, OMG! Today was his birthday! July 31st, and he was…let's see, he had been twenty-five just five years ago, so that must make him….oh shit! THIRTY!

Hairy lay in his waterbed, enshrouded in the darkness that was the basement, and pondered the fact that today was his thirtieth birthday. The age of no return! He kept turning it over and over in his mind. *I am thirty! I am fucking old!* He knew there was no way his aunt was going to bake him a cake. Hell, the Doofuses probably didn't even remember that it was his birthday anyway. *Nobody gives a shit about me.* He thought as he lay there, feeling more and more sorry for himself. Then, as if on cue, Hairy heard a strange commotion coming from upstairs. A noise both distinct and unmistakable.

"Gobble-gobble-gobble."

"What the fuck?" he said aloud. Was that a…turkey? In the house? A goddamn turkey in the house here on Privet Drive? Surely the homeowners association didn't allow such things. Not here. In the stodgiest, most conservative neighborhood in all of England. Of course, there had been that business with the neighbors, the Dursley's, a few years back. Whatever was going on upstairs, Hairy wanted no part of it. He covered his head with his pillow, made no noise and tried to pretend he didn't exist.

"Gobble-gobble-gobble."

There it was again! And much louder than before! He knew it wasn't Thanksgiving or Christmas, the traditional turkey eating holidays. It was July 31st and besides, this was England, they didn't celebrate Thanksgiving like those damn Americans did, anyway. He searched his burned out brain for an answer that made sense. Maybe his Uncle Dagwood was watching one of those nature shows on the telly. His uncle fancied himself something of a manly sort of man but in truth was often mistaken for a flaming homosexual.

"Gobble-gobble-gobble."

Was this going to go on all day? Hairy wondered. It was already well past noon and Hairy didn't usually rise until at least 2PM.

"Is there a turkey in the house?" he called out. But no one answered. Then he remembered. His uncle and aunt had...oh, what the hell did they call those things? Ah, yes. Jobs. Boring, mundane, 9-5 kind of jobs. But not Hairy, no sir! None of that shit for him. He was going places. Yes sir, he was going...

"Gobble-gobble-gobble."

...upstairs! That's where he was going! He just had to see what the fuck was making all the racket! So he dragged himself out of his waterbed, slipped his feet into his Star Wars house slippers and climbed the stairs up to the main floor. As the door opened into the living room, he was met with an astonishing, if not completely unexpected sight. There, sitting on his aunt's sofa, was a large brown turkey with a multi-colored tail.

"Bugger." Hairy said. And if the sight of the turkey wasn't unusual enough, it had, clasped in its beak, (That is what they called those things, wasn't it?) a large envelope. Without even thinking, Hairy said,

"Is that for me?"

"Gobble-gobble-gobble."

(Evidently turkeys did not need to open their beaks to gobble.) Hairy felt a little foolish that he had asked the turkey the question in the first place, but, as if in reply, the bird hopped off the sofa and took a step toward him. Hairy looked around, not knowing what to do. Were turkeys dangerous? Should he plot an escape route in case the bird attacked him? Maybe he could find something to use as a weapon to bludgeon it with. The turkey stopped, just a foot away from Hairy, and stared at him for a moment. Then, it gently laid the envelope at Hairy's feet. Hairy bent over cautiously to pick it up, never losing eye contact with the bird. Sure enough, the envelope was for him, for written on the outside, in emerald green ink, was his name, Hairy Pothead. There was no postage stamp on the envelope, but in its place, in red ink, were the words "Postage Due". Hairy turned the letter over and found a wax seal there, bearing a coat of arms. A large H surrounded by small likenesses of a short, fat, smiling man, a bong, a snake and...what the hell was that fourth image? It might have been some sort of bird maybe...he couldn't tell as it was somewhat deformed. He tore open the envelope and pulled a piece of heavy parchment from it, which read...

HAWGSLEG SCHOOL
Of WIZARDRY and HERBOLOGY

The Boy Who Smoked

Headmaster – Bumbling Dumbass
(Order of Cheech and Chong.)

Dear Mr. Pothead,

Happy 11th Birthday!

Guess what? You're a wizard! Surprise!!!

We are pleased to inform you that you have been accepted to Hawgsleg School of Wizardry and Herbology! The bus will be picking you up for school shortly.

Yours sincerely,

Minnie McGanja
Deputy Head-Mistress

Hairy was stunned. What the hell did all of this really mean? Eleventh birthday? Wizard? Herbology? Postage due? He looked at the turkey. The turkey looked back at him.

"Are you sure you got the right fellow?" he asked.

"Positive," said the turkey. Hairy's jaw dropped.

Chapter One

"You can talk?" he said.

"Can't everyone?" the turkey replied.

"Blimey!" said Hairy.

"Indeed," said the turkey.

"Is there anything else I need to know about you?" Hairy asked.

"My name is Butterball," the turkey, who spoke in a female voice and who would henceforth be referred to as Butterball said, "I will be your companion as well as your primary source of communication while you are a student at Hawgsleg."

"You mean I can't take my cell phone with me?" Hairy asked, bummed at the thought that the minutes he'd just purchased for his phone would go to waste.

"The service is horrible there, anyway," Butterball replied.

"Just where is this Hawgsleg located?" Hairy asked.

"Over the river and across the woods…" Butterball started, "around the mountain and through the meadow…" Hairy thought she was finished, but she wasn't.

"You drive 356 miles on Motorway 6 then make a left turn at Edinburgh."

The Boy Who Smoked

"And that's how you get there?" Hairy asked.

"That will get you downtown. From there you just follow the signs to the castle," Butterball answered.

They began to pack all of Hairy's things, which wasn't a lot, really. A couple pair of worn out jeans, a few old rock band t-shirts with pictures of musicians who had long since checked themselves into rest homes and his one pair of Chuck Taylor tennies.

Of course he also packed his bongs, his rolling papers and his roach clips. He was a dedicated pothead, after all. He pulled his stash from under his pillow. Looking at it made him long to light one up, and, surprisingly, it had the same effect on Butterball.

This whole thing was so surreal. Here he was, on his thirtieth birthday, sitting on his waterbed, smoking dope with a talking turkey (who just happened to be one of those types that could not shut the fuck up when they got wasted), waiting for a bus that was going to take him to some wizard school, really, really far way.

Son of a bitch, he thought. *What the fuck have I gotten myself into?*

Chapter Two

The Hawgsleg Express

Hairy sat on the curb, beside him was his knapsack and his new pal, Butterball. They'd been waiting for what seemed like hours, and Hairy's buzz had worn off.

"They're late," Hairy remarked.

"Yep," Butterball replied, looking at her watch.

"Tell me about Hawgsleg," Hairy said, after a pause.

"Not much to tell," Butterball answered. "It's a thousand year old school for wizards, witches, warlocks and will o' the wisp's. The headmaster is an old burnout named Dumbass who likes to bore students to tears with stories from the old days."

Butterball paused for so long that Hairy thought the turkey had finished, but she was just getting wound up.

"The students at Hawgsleg are divided into four separate houses…distinct groups based on various things like their personalities, dispositions and sexual preferences, by the all-seeing, all-knowing Sorting Sock."

"Sorting Sock?"

"Sure," Butterball continued. "it's an ancient athletic sock with magical properties that allows it to see right into your soul."

"Blimey," Hairy muttered. "Does every new student have to try the Sorting Sock on?"

"Hell yeah!" Butterball said. "Ever since 1523."

"Why that year?" Hairy asked.

"That's the year they invented socks, Hairy. Before that they just played eenie-meenie-miney-moe. But like I was saying, there are four houses at Hawgsleg. The most popular is Huff N' Puff. They represent the party people. Big time stoners, the whole lot of them. Everyone wants to be in Huff N' Puff House. Then there's the Merv Griffindors. This house is named for one of the founders of Hawgsleg, Mervin Griffindor. They're mostly cheesy, game show host types. Nice enough people, but don't let them sell you any vowels. And whatever you do, don't follow them when they tell you to 'Come on down!' " Butterball shuddered at some suppressed memory. Hairy figured it was best not to pursue it.

"Anyway, then there's the Sneaky Snakes. This group is composed of rustlers, cutthroats, murderers, bounty hunters, desperados, mugs, pugs, thugs, nitwits, halfwits, dimwits, vipers, snipers, con men, Indian agents, Mexican bandits, muggers, buggerers, bushwhackers, hornswogglers, horse thieves, bull dykes, train robbers, bank robbers, ass-kickers, shit-kickers and Methodists."

After this, Butterball fell silent.

"Wait!" Hairy exclaimed. "Didn't you say there were four houses?"

"Oh yeah…" Butterball remembered. "The fourth one is…well, shit…I don't remember what it's called. It's the house where they put everyone else."

"Everyone else?" Hairy asked.

"You know. The less interesting, supporting characters who never really contribute to the story in any meaningful way. Supposed to be smart…I think. Or maybe they're all good cooks or something. Hell, I don't know. I think their mascot is some big bird. Maybe THE big bird. You know, the one with the imaginary wooly mammoth. "

It was then that they heard a strange noise, a crack like a car backfiring. In fact, that's exactly what it was. Hairy could make out a cloud of black smoke coming up the street. As it got closer, he realized it was Volkswagen Bus. Lime green, with the words "Hawgsleg Express" painted on the side. It stopped right in front of the spot where they were sitting and the side door opened with a bang. In the driver's seat, located on the right side of the vehicle (remember, this story takes place in England), sat the largest black man that Hairy had ever seen…at least in person anyway. He'd seen black people on the telly of course. Basketball games, football games, America's Most Wanted. This black man was wearing dark glasses and gold chains around his neck. He sized up Hairy and said, "My name's Groovius. Groovius Haggard."

"I don't have any money," Hairy said, instinctively.

"I don't want your money, kid! I'm here to take you to Hawgsleg."

"No shit?" Hairy asked, and the surprised tone in his voice surprised even himself. I mean, after you've met a talking turkey, a black man driving a Volkswagen isn't all that unusual really.

"You're the famous Hairy Pothead, ain'tcha?"

"Yeah," Hairy answered. "Have we met?" He knew it was a dumb question. (As we established previously, he had never seen a real black person before.)

"Everyone knows Hairy Pothead," he said. "Why, you're more famous than Michael Jackson!"

This comparison with the King of Pop reminded Hairy of something he'd read in a book once about black people. They loved to remind anyone who'd listen of their contributions to society and culture. Hairy figured he should play along. He didn't want to offend Groovius.

"Or Aretha Franklin," Hairy said.

"Yeah, her too," Groovius replied. "Or how about Luther Vandross?"

"Certainly," Hairy said. "And let's not forget Whitney Houston."

"I could never forget Whitney Houston and you shouldn't forget Prince either."

"Of course not!" Hairy said, but in truth he had forgotten about Prince, seeing as he hadn't released an album of any significance since Purple Rain. Hairy hoped this would end soon. He wasn't sure he could name any other black people, famous or not.

Well Hairy, are you getting in?" Groovius asked. "We have several other stops to make before we get to Hawgsleg."

Hairy looked down at Butterball who had been noticeably quiet during the previous section of dialogue.

"Butterball, why are you being so noticeably quiet?"

"I think the author forgot I was here," she said. Butterball seemed to possess a unique, magical ability to break what Theatre people referred to as the fourth wall and speak directly to the reader. That's you. Yeah, you, holding this book in your hands. Weird, huh? How do you like the story so far? What's that? You don't like it at all? You don't think I'm much of an author, huh? Well, fuck you. I already have your money, dumbass.

Anyway...

Chapter Two

Hairy and Butterball climbed into the back of the bus as the doors shut behind them and…

IT WAS AMAZING!

The back of the bus seemed huge, cavernous even. Like a big recreation center with couches, chairs, pool tables and even a full bar.

Hairy gasped, "It's bigger on the…"

Groovius interrupted him, "Bigger on the inside, yes. Everyone says that when they first get on. Now, sit down!"

"But how?" Hairy asked.

"It's magic, Hairy," Groovius replied. "And this is just the beginning."

Hairy looked around. Several people were already seated on the bus. Most of them seemed to be about Hairy's age.

Whew, Hairy thought, *maybe I'm not the only student who got their invitation nineteen years late!* With Butterball tucked neatly under his arm, he sat down beside a gaunt, red-haired fellow who had a black smudge on his nose.

"What's up?" Hairy asked.

"Not much," the other guy replied. "Is that your turkey?"

"Yeah, I guess so," said Hairy.

"Damn straight I'm his turkey!" Butterball said, holding up a magazine about turkeys and ignoring them.

"I wish I had a turkey. All my family could afford was this." He pulled a rock from his pocket and held it out for Hairy to see.

"That's a rock." Hairy said.

"Bloody hell, I know it's a rock," The red-haired fellow snapped. "I call him Rock Hudson. You know, after that movie star."

"The one that died of AIDS?" Hairy asked. "Did he?"

"I think so," Hairy answered. "It was all over the telly."

"Ain't got no telly. Can't afford one."

There was an awkward pause. Hairy hoped he hadn't offended the fellow, because, truth be told, Hairy was poor himself, or so he believed. Finally, Hairy said, "My name's Hairy Pothead. Pleased to meet you."

The other boy did a double take.

"THE Hairy Pothead?"

"You've heard of me?" Hairy asked, wonderingly.

"Why, yes, I should say so. You are rather famous, aren't you?"

Chapter Two

"Am I?" Hairy asked, even more wonderingly.

"My name's Red Measley, but you can just call me Red," Red said, introducingly.

"Red it is, then." Hairy said, liking this guy more and more. And so, as the Hawgsleg Express puttered along up the road, the two boys continued their conversation. Red came from a very large, Mormon, wizard family. His father, Archie Measley, actually worked for the wizarding government, studying Fuglies. (That was what magic people called regular non-magic people.)

His mother, Little Orphan Annie Measley, stayed home to raise their red-haired brood. Red had five older brothers. Carrot Top, his oldest brother, had once been a moderately famous prop comic. His brother, Rouge, worked abroad (and sometimes two broads when he was really lucky!) in the Red Dragon District. Prissy, whose name, although not indicative of his flaming red hair, was appropriate for other reasons. Then there were the twins, Heathcliff and Garfield. They were the practical joking, alley catting, ne'er-do-wells of the Measley family. Then there was Red and last but not least, his younger sister,

Ginger, who wouldn't start school until next year.

"Is she hot?" Hairy asked, without thinking. After all, he hadn't gotten laid since... *Oh my God! Had it really been that long???*

"Dude, that's my little sister!" Red yelled.

"She's like twenty-nine, right?" Hairy retorted. "What's the big deal?"

"Will you two quit your prattling? I'm trying to read." The voice had come from the couch behind them. Hairy and Red looked around to see who had spoken. There stood an attractive young woman with a head full of curly hair and a pair of tits that would keep you awake at night in contemplation.

"Bugger," Red said. "Who are you supposed to be?"

The girl looked down the end of her nose at them, sniffed and said, "I'm Hornie Stranger and if the two of you could keep your voices down, I might be able to get some studying done."

"Studying?" asked Hairy. "But school hasn't even started yet."

"I'm trying to get a head start. Oh, and you have a smudge on your nose, dumbass," she said looking at Red with disgust. And with that, she sat back down and held up a book between her and the two of them.

"Bloody hell, did you see the tits on her, mate?" Red whispered, rubbing the dirt off his nose.

"Kind of bookish though, isn't she?" Hairy replied in kind.

"I'd still hit that." Red said, feeling deep down inside that someday, he would.

Hairy noticed that three figures were approaching them: a snow white haired man in a black suit, flanked by two bigger men who reminded Hairy of gargoyles, only uglier. The white haired man walked right up and leaned in to Hairy, getting so close to him that the tips of their noses touched.

"Uh...hi," Hairy said, apprehensively, feeling like he ought to say something.

"Hairy Pothead?" The white haired man asked.

"Yeah," Hairy replied.

"Looks more like Hairy Shithead to me," the man said, sneeringly. His two companions snickered.

"That's a good one," the goon on the left said.

"Yeah, a good one," the other thug said, sounding like an over-grown parrot. Neither of them appeared to be too bright to Hairy. They moved on to a couch near the back of the bus.

"What's his problem?" Hairy asked, staring after them; they returned his staring by making grotesque faces.

"That's Drago Malfeasance. He comes from one of the richest and most powerful wizarding families in the entire Wizarding World. The other two are his pals, Crabs and Herpes."

"Which is which?" Hairy inquired.

"Does it matter?" Red countered.

But of course it didn't. It was then that the bus stopped suddenly and everyone toppled over each other.

"Sorry," Groovius called out. "We're here."

"Where's here?" Hairy asked, pulling himself up off the ground.

"The only place where young wizards and witches like yourselves can find all the books, robes, and wands that you will need for a year at school without spending a bloody fortune…Wal-Mart."

Chapter Three

The Wizard of Wal-Mart

"Wal-Mart?" Hairy asked, puzzled. "They sell magic supplies?"

"Hairy," Groovius stated, "Wal-Mart sells everything."

And so they all got out of the micro-bus and walked through the automatic doors. An unnaturally short, elderly gentleman greeted them as they entered, following in Groovius' large wake.

"That guy was unnaturally short and elderly, huh?" Hairy remarked to Groovius in an undertone.

"Well, Hairy," Groovius said in the same tone. "Not a lot of people know this, but Wal-Mart is run by goblins. Very possessive and untrusting. You would be crazy to try and steal anything from them."

"I always suspected that there was something strange about the employees here," Hairy replied, looking back at the greeter, who leered nastily at him. Hairy shuddered as he continued, "And no worries, I already know what happens when you take stuff from Wal-Mart. Hey, where's the wizarding stuff at anyway?"

"In the Wizarding Department...duh," Drago sneered.

"Yeah, duh," Crabs repeated.

"Yeah, duh," Echoed Herpes.

Hairy had already decided he didn't like these three. By now, they were in the middle of the store, where, sure enough, there was a sign hanging from the ceiling that read "WIZARDING DEPARTMENT".

Hairy leaned over to Red, speaking quietly, "I've been to Wal-Mart a million times and I've never been in this department."

"I've never been in the women's maxi-pads," Red replied. "But I'm pretty sure the department exists."

Hairy couldn't argue this point.

Chapter Three

"The Wizarding Department only appears to those who need it," Groovius announced to the group, making Hairy wonder if he'd overheard their conversation. "Now, get what you need, and we'll be on our way…"

Before he could finish speaking, an announcement come over the store's PA system, "Security cameras, please focus all cameras on the Wizarding Department."

Hairy knew this announcement had been directed at Groovius, but he didn't seem to take any notice so Hairy wasn't going to make an issue of it either. The students spread out, picking up various items off the shelves and putting them in their carts.

"I have no idea what I'm doing," Hairy told Red. "I don't know what I need."

"The usual stuff," Red said. "Robes, books, yams, and a magic wand. What kind of wizard are you anyway?"

"I'm not a wizard at all!" Hairy protested.

"But you're the famous Hairy Pothead!" Red insisted.

"Why does everyone keep calling me that?" Hairy asked, exasperated.

"What?"

"Famous. Why does everyone keep calling me famous?"

"Because…you are. Look…" With that, Red picked a book up off the shelf and handed it to Hairy. There, on the cover, much to his surprise was a picture of his face.

"I'll be goddamned!" Hairy exclaimed. It was a good picture, a recent one from the looks of it, though for the life of him, he couldn't remember even posing for it. The book's title, in big bold letters read, "The Famous Hairy Pothead by JK Rowling".

"I didn't know someone had written a book about me!" Hairy said.

"Oh, yeah," Red said. "There's a whole bunch of them. See?" Red pointed to a shelf on which numerous books were displayed, all of them about Hairy. There was "Hairy Pothead: The Stoned Sorcerer," "Hairy Pothead and the Secret Chamberpot," "Hairy Pothead and the Prison Ass Banger," "Hairy Pothead: The Fire Gobbler," "Hairy Pothead and the Order of Roast Turkey on Rye," "Hairy Pothead and the Half Ass Sequel," and "Hairy Pothead and the Greedy Author, Parts 1 And 2".

"I'll be a son of a bitch!" Hairy exclaimed. "I AM famous!"

Chapter Three

"Told you so," said Red, "and if you think that's something, you should see all the merchandise!" Red picked up a coffee mug with Hairy's likeness on it and a t-shirt…in fact, there were tons of items with Hairy's picture and name on them. There were placemats, action figures, posters, and his picture was even on a box of macaroni and cheese, with noodles that were shaped like a pot leaf.

"How did all of this happen?" Hairy asked.

"Read the first book," Red suggested. "It's the shortest of the lot. A pretty easy read really."

Hairy put the book in his cart and continued his shopping. He picked up some other books that Red said he would need, a wizard robe, deodorant, toothpaste, a couple of yams, and proceeded to the wand aisle.

There were literally thousands of wands to choose from of every size and color. Hairy thought they all resembled dildos…and they did.

"The selection of a wand," Groovius began, "is one of the most important choices in determining how successful you'll be at Hawgsleg and in your careers thereafter. Most

believe that a wizard does not actually choose
his or her wand, but that the wand itself
chooses the wizard. I think its all horseshit
myself...but choose carefully, just in case."

Hairy made his way down the aisle and
halfway down, he picked up a pink wand. He
looked it over, and then shook it. It began to
get warm and, much to Hairy's surprise, started
to vibrate. Hairy hastily sat it back on the shelf,
looking over his shoulder to see if anyone was
watching. Sure enough, Drago, Crabs, and
Herpes were looking right at him, pointing and
laughing. Hairy moved around to another aisle
to get away from them. There was no one in
the next aisle, except for an old bearded man
wearing a blue Wal-Mart vest. He seemed to be
straightening up the merchandise on the
shelves. Hairy looked at the wands on the
shelves, but nothing caught his eye.

"Looking for a wand?" Hairy jumped,
surprised to see the old man was standing next
to him. Hairy hadn't even noticed him
approaching. Hairy was also startled by the old
man's eyes which were a color he had never
seen before. Silver, like the moon.

"Uh, yeah…" Hairy replied, shortly, not at all interested in starting a conversation with the old man in the middle of the (dildo) aisle.

"They say the wand chooses the wizard," the old man said, obviously not taking the hint.

"That's what I've heard," Hairy said, not making eye contact. They really did freak him out.

"I've got what you want," the old man said. Hairy paused. The old man continued, "I've got what you want right here, boy."

Hairy couldn't help but notice the old man patting himself on the front pocket of his pants, where, to Hairy's horror, there was a large bulge.

"No thanks!" Hairy said, and quickly moved to another aisle, but upon entering encountered the old man again. *How had he gotten there so fast?*

"It's the perfect fit," the old man said. Hairy switched aisles once more, but was again greeted by the old letch.

"Leave me alone!" Hairy cried, beginning to run from aisle to aisle only to find the old man there waiting for him every time. Finally, Hairy gave up. The old man walked up to him, and Hairy prepared for the worst.

"This is what you've been looking for," the old fellow said, and with that, he pulled what looked like a long black dong out of his pocket.

"Oh, God!" Hairy exclaimed. "Are you going to use that on me...with no lube?"

"What?" said the old man. "Why would I use your own wand on you?"

"Wand?" Hairy asked, still terrified at the thought of being violated without proper preparation.

"This is your wand, Hairy. It's part of a set, the other being wielded by you know...WHO."

"Who?" Hairy asked, swearing that he had heard owls hooting somewhere in the store.

"Exactly," the old man said, placing the wand in Hairy's hand. Hairy looked it over and was surprised to find that something about it just felt...right. It was the right size. Not too big or too small. It was black as night and felt soft to the touch...like...skin. Hairy knew that somehow this wand had been made just for him.

"Remember Hairy, it isn't about how big it is...it's how you use it."

Hairy waved the wand in the air...nothing happened. He did it again. Still nothing...he must be doing it wrong. He carefully took the wand in his left hand and stroked it from base to tip with his right. A feeling of elation coursed through him like a pleasant stream of electricity. He stroked it again, paying closer attention to the tip and again he felt the electric pleasure shoot through his whole body. He continued to stroke it, faster and faster, harder and harder, hardly aware of what he was doing as pleasure built up in every fiber of his being until the point where he thought he would explode…

"Hairy?"

He stopped all movement, and opened his eyes. (When had he closed them?) He was surrounded by Groovius and all the other students. Drago and his goons were giggling at him. The old man was nowhere to be found.

"Hairy?" Groovius repeated. "I take it you've found a wand?"

"Actually," Hairy said, "the wand chose me."

"Horseshit," Groovius scoffed.

Chapter Four

Hawgsleg

The group of students made their way to the front of the store with their purchases in hand. Hairy grew worried as they approached the check-out lines about how he was going to pay for all of his supplies. As if reading his mind, Groovius handed him a gold Britannica Express card, saying, "Pay for your stuff with this."

"Huh?" Hairy said, stupidly. "I don't have any money. Where did this come from?"

"Actually, you're rich, Hairy. You've been earning royalties on all the books and merchandise since you were eleven. The money has been deposited into this account for you and has earned a shitload of interest."

Chapter Four

Hairy could only gape. Rich? Him? His mind whirled with all the possibilities. He was going to buy enough Wacky Backy to last a lifetime!

Their purchases paid for, the group got back on the bus. After a brief stop to pick up some smoke, they were on their way to Hawgsleg. Hairy was excited. He'd had very little to look forward to in a long time. As the bus sped through the night, Hairy drifted off to sleep, dreaming of dime bags and big booties.

He awoke as the sun was rising between the mountains. Hairy looked out the window and what he saw nearly took his breath away.

It was a large gray castle, imposing to say the least, partially because the main section of the castle resembled a large skull.

"Now that's fucking cool!" Hairy shouted. The other students must have agreed, because their reaction was a collective oooh, ahhh, wow, etc. As they approached, a large wooden drawbridge lowered over the moat, allowing the bus to drive over it and into the skull's mouth.

There was a crazy amount of flurried activity within the castle as other students were arriving. Some in buses, some flying on broomsticks and still others appearing out of what looked like outdoor fireplaces in a rush of emerald green flames. Hairy and the others stepped out of the bus. A short, fat woman walked up to the group.

"Greetings. I trust your journey was pleasant."

She was a wearing a pointy black hat. Hairy assumed she must be a witch.

"My name is Minnie McGanja. I am the Deputy Headmistress here at Hawgsleg and the Wicked Witch of the West. Do any of you have any questions?"

Every single one of them raised their hand.

McGanja sighed and said, "The bathroom is down the corridor, to the left."

After they had relieved themselves, they gathered in a great hall. At a long table at the front of the room was seated a motley crew of colorful characters...well, more ZZ Top than motley crew really. Seated at the center was an ancient looking wizard. Hairy assumed the old man must be the one Butterball had told him about, the headmaster, Dumbass. The man stood and held up his arms as the room went silent. He lowered his arms and the noise rose again, louder than before. He raised them again, and immediately silence fell.

"I love that shit," he said, stepping forward to address the crowd. "My name is Bumbling Archibald Edwin Quincy Xanadu Elizabeth Dumbass, but you may call me PROFESSOR Dumbass."

There was a smattering of snickers. Dumbass ignored them, or possible didn't hear them at all. He looked like he was about 600 years old. He was in fact, only 572. He continued.

"I would like to welcome you to the Hawgsleg School of Wizardry and Herbology. Founded for the continuing education of wizards, witches, warlocks and will o' the wisps. I must apologize for the lateness of your invitations. You see, like other, better funded wizarding schools, it has always been our intention to begin your training at the age of eleven. However, because of budget cuts, we have been forced to use turkeys as our mode of delivering school letters, and turkeys, while being quite tasty (especially with cranberry sauce!) are...slow. Very slow. But as they say, better late than transmuted into a toad!"

"Do people actually say that?" Hairy asked in a whisper. "Because I have never heard that."

"Shut up!" Hornie whispered behind him. Hairy refocused on the headmaster as he continued his speech.

"And now, before we go any further, I'd like to introduce you to the faculty. First, I'd like you to meet Deputy Headmistress, Minnie McGanja." She stood up and acknowledged the hearty applause from the students. "Professor of Transmutation, Teleportation, Transfiguration and Show Choir." McGanja sat back down.

"Next, Professor Squirrel." A smallish man wearing an enormous turban stood up. He appeared to be very nervous about something.

"He teaches our Dark Art Class, specifically painting on black velvet." Squirrel sat down, backwards for some reason.

"This is Professor Twig." A woman, covered in mud and dirt stood. "She teaches hydroponics and Broomsticks." Twig returned to her seat.

"This is our teacher of Lucky Charms, Professor Dopey." A very small man climbed up in his chair to be seen over the table.

"I know what you people are thinking," Professor Dopey said. "And I am not a Goddamn Leprechaun. I'm a dwarf. So don't be asking to see me pot of fucking gold!"

"Thank you, Professor Dopey," Dumbass said, as Dopey took his seat. "That was very colorful. And, of course, last but not least...our Professor of Herbology...say, where is he?"

At that moment, the lights in the hall went out, and creepy organ music began to play that reminded Hairy of something out of Dracula or Phantom of the Opera. The doors to the great hall opened and a tall, dark man stood silhouetted in the doorway.

"Ah, yes," Dumbass continued. "There he is...Professor Rape. Severe-Ass Rape." Everyone in the hall immediately gasped and grabbed their asses.

"Did he say Ass Rape?" Hairy asked.

"Severe-Ass Rape," Red answered.

"Bollocks," Hairy said.

"Could someone turn the lights back on, please?" Dumbass asked, and with that, the lights came back on. Professor Rape took his place at the table.

"Can we get a round of applause for our faculty, please?" Dumbass flourished his wand

and the sound of canned applause filled the air. A few students joined in, unenthusiastically.

"And now, as is our tradition here at Hawgsleg, we will sort of each of you into one of the four houses. For this, we will need the…" He flourished his wand again and the sound of a drum roll could be heard. "Sorting Sock!"

There was a pause.

"The Sorting Sock!"

Another pause.

"Can someone please bring me the damn Sorting Sock?"

McGanja stood and walked around the table to Dumbass, whispering something in his ear.

"Oh!" He said. "I forgot."

Dumbass bent over, took his boot off and removed a long white tube sock from his foot. He held it up in the air.

"I put it on for safe keeping." He informed them all, placing the Sock on his hand like a sock puppet. Suddenly, the Sock seemed to come to life and a deep, masculine voice spoke.

"Feed me."

"Not now." Dumbass replied.

"Feed me."

"Later."

"Feed me."

"After the ceremony."

"Whatever."

Red leaned over to Hairy.

"The Sorting Sock always begins the ceremony with a bit of advice for the coming school year. Very heavy stuff."

"I am the all-seeing, all-knowing Sorting Sock," the Sock began, "and I offer you these words of wisdom…" There was a long pause.

"WASH YOUR MOTHER FUCKING FEET! What the hell's the matter with you people? You think I enjoy getting put on a hundred damn dirty feet every year? There…I'm finished."

"You sure?" Dumbass asked.

"Yeah. I'm fine. Get on with it." The Sock replied.

McGanja brought a chair forward, placing it front and center.

"When I call your name," she said, "please come forward to be sorted. First, Hornie Stranger."

Hornie stepped to the front of the room, and removed her shoe, a Mary Jane. Dumbass placed the Sock on her small foot. It moved from side to side, slowly at first, but then faster and faster. Finally it proclaimed...

"MERV GRIFFINDOR!"

The table on the far left applauded loudly.

"That can't be right!" Hornie protested."I'm too smart for Griffindor!"

"I'm sorry, my dear," Dumbass said. "The Sock is never wrong."

"Never?"

"Hardly ever."

"But then…"

"NEXT!"

Dumbass roughly pulled the Sock off Hornie's foot. She huffed and puffed and moved off to sit at the Merv Griffindor table.

"Drago Malfeasance!" McGanja called out.

He came forward, and sat in the chair, removing his very expensive loafers.

"Let's get this over with." Drago sneered.

"Well, aren't you a ray of sunshine?" Dumbass asked, sarcastically.

"Fuck off, old man." Drago spat.

Dumbass threw the Sock at Drago, hitting him in the eye. Drago spluttered in indignation and put the Sock on his foot.

"Uggg!" said the Sock.

Chapter Four

"My feet are clean, you worthless piece of hosiery!" Drago exclaimed.

"Some funk can't be washed off with soap and water," the Sock responded. "This one is easy…SNEAKY SNAKE!"

The table on the far right of the hall hissed loudly.

"Big surprise," Dumbass commented.

Drago threw him a dirty look, picked up his shoe and tossing his white hair out of his eyes, walked to his seat.

"Red Measley."

Red stepped forward and sat in the chair. He removed his shoe and placed the Sock upon his foot.

"Not another damn Measley!" the Sock said. "How many more of you are there?"

"Just me and my sister," Red said.

"Damn, don't you people believe in birth control?" the Sock said.

"Beg pardon?" Red said.

"Never mind. Let's see. All the Measley's before you were in Griffindor, right?"

"Yes."

"But you, you're a precocious little shit, aren't you?"

"That's what my mum always says."

"I think I'll shake things up a bit this time. Put you in Huff N Puff."

"What?" Red said, nearly jumping out of his seat. "Really?"

"No," the Sock replied. "I was just shitting you, kid. MERV GRIFFINDOR!"

There was another round of applause from the Griffindor table as Red returned to his seat.

"Hairy Pothead!" McGanja's voice rang out. What little noise was in the hall died at once as everyone's attention became focused on the front of the room. Hairy found it hard to swallow as his mouth suddenly became very dry. He walked to the front of the room, and sat on the chair. He removed his Chucks, which seemed to take longer than usual with his hands shaking. Dumbass reverently placed the Sock on his foot.

"Hmmm…" said the Sock. "Curious…very curious. This is most unusual."

"What is?"

"I could easily put you in the Sneaky Snake House, Hairy. You certainly have a devious side."

"Doesn't everyone?" Hairy asked.

45

Chapter Four

"Sure, sure." the Sock replied. "But I need to put you with Hornie and Red, so you can have adventures together."

"Why is that?" Hairy asked.

"That's just the way these stories go. If this process made any sense at all, Red would be in Huff N Puff and Hornie with that other group...the bird one with all the smart kids...No, my choice is clear...MERV GRIFFINDOR!"

The Merv Griffindor table went wild with applause and cheers for no apparent reason. Hairy put his shoe back on and went to sit at the table near Hornie. Hairy was in a state of shock and so, conveniently didn't pay much attention to where the other students were placed. It was hard to believe how much his life had changed in the last twenty four hours. He'd been nothing more than a lovable, poorly-groomed, under-achieving stoner, but now he was a lovable, poorly-groomed, under-achieving, stoner WIZARD! He wondered to himself what adventure awaited him in the next year. Of course he had the book about his first year in his back pocket. Should he look at it? Could it predict what was going to happen to him here at Hawgsleg? It was a lot to consider.

Hawgsleg

Hairy couldn't wait to get checked into his room and hit the bong!

Chapter Five

Who?

In fact, he didn't wait, slipping out of the large hall to light up old Betsy in the men's room. He'd scarcely taken his first puff when he heard moaning coming from the stall next to him.

"Got one stuck in there sideways?" He asked.

The moaning increased.

"Bear down and give that turd hell!!"

Suddenly a head poked through the wall and into Hairy's stall, followed by a ghostly body.

"Holy shit!" Hairy said. "You're a ghost!"

"How'd you guess?" The ghost said.

"Because you're wearing a sheet with two eye holes cut out of it." Hairy answered and indeed, the ghost was dressed like a cliché.

Who?

"It's a classic look," the ghost replied. "But why aren't you afraid of me?"

"Dude. I'm a stoner. I've seen way scarier shit than you."

"I guess that makes sense," the ghost agreed.

"You wanna hit this with me?" Hairy asked.

"Hell yeah," said the ghost and he did. They smoked for the better part of the hour. Hairy learned that the ghost's name was Mostly Bodiless Merl. He'd been a wandering minstrel nearly 500 years before. But one day, after smoking a particularly good bowl, he'd wandered a little too far into the forest where he'd been eaten by a group of hungry forest creatures. He was cursed to roam the halls of Hawgsleg as a ghost until he collected enough community service hours to allow him to cross over to the other side.

In fact, there were a lot of ghosts here at Hawgsleg in the same position. One in particular that intrigued Hairy was Fertile Myrtle, a ghost so horny, according to Merl, she'd fuck anyone. Dead or alive.

"That doesn't sound so bad," Hairy said, after Merl had described her.

Chapter Five

"Young fellow," Merl began, "Have you ever been fucked by a poltergeist?"

"Can't say as I have." Hairy answered. "Why? Is it awesome?"

"Absolutely not," Merl said. "If you think living women are clingy, try getting away from a woman who can follow you ANYWHERE...FOR FUCKING EVER!"

"Just how many community service hours do you have to do?" Hairy asked.

"A bajillion."

"A bajillion?"

"Yep."

"Is that even a real number?"

"Oh, yes," Merl answered. "Pretty much any number you can imagine is a real number."

"It just seems like a lot."

"Not so much, when you're a ghost," Merl replied. "Time isn't as big a deal."

"Is there any other way for you to cross over?" Hairy asked. "Other than serving a bajillion community service hours?"

Merl thought about it for a moment, "I suppose if all my remains were to be brought together and given a proper burial, that would be enough to break the curse, and allow me to enter the after world but it would be rather

Who?

difficult as they were devoured by seven different creatures…almost 500 years ago."

There was a pause.

"Yeah, probably not much chance," Hairy said but he had another idea. Perhaps Merl could help him out during his first school year and earn some community service hours that way. After all, Hairy was totally clueless about what he was doing at Hawgsleg and he could use all the help he could get. He explained his idea to Merl and the ghost seemed excited by the prospect.

"The most important thing I can tell you, Hairy, is to be on guard against…you know…WHO."

Again. Hairy could swear he heard the hooting of owls, even here, in the castle.

"Who?" Hairy asked.

"Precisely."

"Wait!" Hairy said. "Who?"

"You know."

"No, I don't."

"You don't? Really?"

"Really. I don't."

"You faced him before, Hairy."

"Who?"

"Indeed."

"No. Who did I face?"

"King Owl Jr.," Merl whispered. "WHO."

"Who?"

"Yes. That's what they call him. WHO."

Hairy was growing tired of the Abbot and Costello routine.

"Who is King Owl Jr.?" He asked.

"He's the Owl King," Merl replied. "The most evil being who ever existed." His tone took on that of someone telling a ghost story. Ironic considering he was a ghost.

"I've never heard of this King Owl Jr.," Hairy said.

"Shhhh," Merl cautioned. "People are afraid of saying his name out loud, Hairy. Afraid he'll hear it and think someone is calling him. Do you hear those owls hooting right now? When they hear his name being called they start doing that and if they do it enough, he will appear and that…WOULD BE VERY, VERY BAD! Most people just refer to him simply as WHO. I suppose your relatives didn't think it was important to tell you about the one who killed your parents. Typical fuglies. Typical, typical, typical."

"You said I faced him, but I don't recall that at all," Hairy said.

Who?

"You were just a little blighter," Merl said. "Mewling in your crib. He's the one who offed your mum and dad."

"What?" Hairy said, standing up. "What the hell are you talking about? My parents died in a freak Cuisinart accident."

"Horseshit, Hairy!" Merl exclaimed, "That's a bunch of horseshit. Who told you that rubbish?"

"My aunt and uncle."

"Figures. Fuglies didn't want you to know the truth."

"Bollocks, Merl. What is the truth?"

"They were offed by King...err...WHO."

"But why?" Hairy asked. "I always figured my parents were a sweet little couple who never did anything wrong."

"BWAH-HA-HA-HA-HA!" Merl's laugh was somewhat obnoxious. "Oh, no, kid. Your parents were great, they really were, but they weren't saints or nothing. Fact is, Jack and Jill grew some of the best weed in the whole country. Your mom was a genius at growing the stuff."

Could it be true? Hairy wondered. His parents had been stoners like himself! After all these years of being told what tee-totalers his

53

parents had been and feeling like he could never measure up, he was finally hearing the truth about them. And he liked what he was hearing...except the part about them being killed.

"Why'd he kill them?" Hairy queried.

"Why do you think, kid? They were cutting in on his action."

"And you said I had faced him. What was that all about?"

"When you were a wee lad, Hairy. He tried to cast the Killing Curse on you, but it didn't take."

"Killing Curse?" Hairy asked. "What's that?"

"It's the worst curse of all, Hairy. And nothing that you should be worrying about right now. You'll learn about it in your classes, later."

"Wow," Hairy said. "I never knew any of this shit."

"I reckon not," Merl said. "Your aunt and uncle are a couple of douche bags."

"I agree."

"He knows you've come to Hawgsleg, Hairy. You're safe here for the most part, but take care. He wants to get his hands on you and your special magic."

"My special magic? What's that?"

"That mark on your head," Merl said. Hairy brushed his hair aside, revealing the cannabis leaf imprinted there.

"You mean this?"

"It's magic, Hairy. Powerful magic from your parents," Merl explained.

"What's it do?" Hairy asked.

"Nobody knows, but there are those, Dumbass especially, who believe it'll reveal itself at the proper time and place."

"This is some heavy shit," Hairy murmured, and indeed it was.

Chapter 6

Herbology Class

The next morning Hairy had his first class at Hawgsleg, Herbology with Rape. There was something about this professor that sent chills up Hairy's spine. Maybe it was his name. Severe-Ass Rape just didn't sound pleasant, even if you said it with a big smile on your face.

Try it. Seriously. Right now. I'll pause the book while you smile a big shit eating grin and say SEVERE-ASS RAPE. There. See what I mean?

Anyway...it wasn't just Rape's name that bothered Hairy. There was something... frighteningly familiar about Rape. About the way he looked into Hairy's eyes whenever they passed in the hall, or at mealtimes, or any time they were in the same room together! The evening before they had passed each other and Rape's glare was so intense he'd walked into a wall. It would have been funnier to Hairy if Rape hadn't deducted 10,000 points from the Merv Griffindors out of anger and embarrassment.

Points were given by the staff of Hawgsleg for doing something positive and likewise deducted if a house member or members fucked up. The house that had attained the most points by the end of the school year won the House Cup, a great, big, gold trophy. To Hairy, the whole thing seemed arbitrary and pointless. Each of the staff members had been students at Hawgsleg once upon a time and it was no secret that each of them favored their own house. Rape had been a Sneaky Snake (big fucking surprise there). Dumbass had been a Merv Griffendor, as had McGanja. Maybe they would help make up the 10,000 points that Hairy had already lost his house.

Hairy was seated between Red and Hornie as Rape entered, throwing the door open so hard that it banged off the wall.

"Shut your fucking mouths and take out your books. I want you to read chapters 1-25."

Chapter Six

Rape sneered at them without preamble, his voice a low hiss. Yep, definitely a Sneaky Snake.

"What the hell?" Hairy said, out loud. Everyone turned and looked at him, including Rape.

"Do you have a problem with the assignment, Mr. Pothead?" There was no mistaking the venom in his voice.

"That seems like a lot of work." Hairy said. "For the first day, I mean."

"Perhaps you don't need to do the reading, Mr. Pothead? Perhaps you already know everything there is to know about HERBOLOGY!"

The last word came out as a sudden yell and the entire class jumped. The room was still.

Herbology? Was he talking about growing pot? Hairy wondered. Because truth be told, Hairy was pretty knowledgeable about that particular subject.

"Actually, Professor Rape," Hairy said. "I am pretty knowledgeable about that particular subject."

The class gasped as one at Hairy's boldness.

"Oh ho!" Rape exclaimed. "Did you hear that class? Mr. Pothead fancies himself something of an expert on the subject of herbs. Tell me, Mr. Pothead, how did you come to be such a learned expert?"

"Well," Hairy explained. "I've been growing my own herbs in the basement for years."

"And you think that makes you an expert, Mr. Pothead?" Rape was getting angry and Hairy wasn't so sure he was going to make it to the end of his first day a school. Rape continued, "If you are such an expert, perhaps you wouldn't mind answering a few questions for the class?"

"Uh...sure." Hairy said, in a bemused tone.

"Let's make this interesting, shall we?" Rape said with a smirk. "If Mr. Pothead gets all the questions right, then every one of you may skip the first twenty-five chapters. It's all hogwash, anyway."

Everyone looked around at each other with puzzled faces, not sure what to make of Rape's offer.

"IF... however, Mr. Pothead gets one question wrong, then the assignment will be tripled."

Holy shit, Hairy thought. *What have I done now?* The students all shot Hairy a hateful look. He'd better not fuck up or he'd never live this down.

"Name sixty-one kinds of marijuana," Rape said.

"Oh bugger," Red said, under his breath. "We're all fucked."

Hairy only grinned.

"There are many types or strains of marijuana," he began. "However, they basically fit into two categories; Indica and Sativa. Breeders often cross different strains to change the growing methods or properties of the original."

Hairy stood, his confidence growing.

"As a rule of thumb, Indicas tend to be shorter, stockier plants with smaller, denser and smellier buds. Indicas also flower much faster than Sativas, usually with a 6-9 week flowering period. Sativas will grow taller and generally much bigger. Their buds will also be bigger but much less dense. Sativa buds will also be less smelly and take longer to flower than Indicas, usually 9-10 weeks."

He thought about lighting one up, but that seemed like a bit much.

"Choosing types of marijuana for your crop will depend on many factors, not the least of which is what you expect of the end product. Marijuana strains are often a cross of Sativa and Indica to give properties of each to make certain Sativa smaller and more potent, or an Indica larger and with bigger buds. As far as the high you get from smoking them is concerned, Sativas will tend to produce more of a cerebral, energetic or giggly high, while Indicas produce more of a stoned feeling, known to enhance physical aspects such as sound and taste and if I may say so myself, Professor Rape, can also have a very relaxing effect."

He paused, and as he did, Rape started to say something. Hairy cut him off.

"As to sixty-one varieties of marijuana, my answer is Early Girl, Early Misty, Fourway, Hawaii Mauwie Wauwie, Hawaii Skunk, Hawaii x Skunk 1, Haze19 x Skunk, Haze, Hindu Kush, Hollands Hope, Ice, Ice 2003, Indoor Mix, Island Lady, Jack Herrer, Jack Horror, K2, Khola, Mango, Maroc x Afghan, Maroc x Skunk Special, Master Kush, Master Kush x Northern Lights, Mauwie Wauwie, Mazar, Misty, Mixed Sativa, Natural Mystic, New Purple Power, Nigeria, Northern Lights, Northern Lights x Big Bud, Northern Lights x

Chapter Six

Haze, Northern Lights x Shiva, Orange Bud, Papaya, PPP Feminized, Purple Power, PPP, Shiva, Silver Haze, Skunk, Skunk Red Hair, Skunk Special, Snow White, Super Girl, Super Skunk, Swazi, Swazi x Skunk, Swiss Miss, Thai x Skunk, Top44, Turtle Power, Venus, White Rhino and White Widow."

The room was silent for what seemed like forever.

"Too easy," Rape finally broke the silence. "Any stoner could do that with ease."

"Any stoner who was awesome," Hairy said, smirking.

"So smug aren't you Pothead? Just like your father," Rape sneered, full of hatred.

Wait. What had Rape meant by that? Had Rape known his father? They would be about the same age. It would make sense that they would have attended Hawgsleg at about the same time.

"Next question," Rape continued. "What is the best strain of marijuana for medical use?"

Medical use? Hairy thought. That was a tough one and of course, that is exactly what Rape had intended it to be. Hairy was a stoner. What could he possibly know about medical marijuana, right? Hairy tried to clear his pot addled brain for the answer. Thinking about THC levels and harvest times. He did some quick calculations.

"Naught plus naught equals naught," he muttered.

"Don't stall!" Rape spat. "What is your answer?"

"It's a trick question." Hairy said.

"Hardly, Mr. Pot…"Rape began, but Hairy cut him off. "There is much debate among the experts as to which strain IS the best for medical use, but many agree that White Rhino is certainly one of the best. It's an excellent cross of White Widow and a powerful Indica strain and is VERY high in THC which makes it good for medical use. White Rhino has a sweet, slightly hashy taste, which makes it ideal for bonging. If you don't believe me, I have some back in my room."

Several of the students stifled giggles at this.

"You see, due to the Indica cross, White Rhino is denser and shorter than White Widow, with very white crystals, kind of like Drago's hair."

At that, he reached over and mussed up Drago's white locks. Drago looked pissed.

Chapter Six

"White Rhino seeds are excellent for medical marijuana applications."

"Damn it," Rape muttered, as the class let out a cheer. Rape shot them a look that said SHUT THE FUCK UP. They did. He stared into Hairy' eyes intently.

"Wassup Jack?" He said in a language the students had never heard before. "Let me pinch an inch of ya stash or ain't you chill wid a brutha?"

Almost without thinking Hairy replied, "I'm chill but a brutha better step off fo I bust a cap in his mudda fuggin ass."

Rape was shocked so much by Hairy's response that he literally stepped back.

"Don't blow yo wig, Jack. I ain't coming on that tab, dig?"

"I dig." Hairy replied.

"You're a hip cat, ain't ya? You really got your boots on, hell you best not be cabbaging all up in my bizness or I be runnin' cold upside down yo nappy ass head, you dig?"

"Hey homey, I dig yo rap, and I don't want no piece. Dig that?"

"I say hey, s'other say I won say. I pray to J, I get the same ol, same ol."

"Knock yourself a strike, pro Playa. Gray matter back got to perform us, down I take TCB in, man."

"You know wha' they say Bro: See a broad to get the booty. Lay 'em down an smack 'em yack 'em."

"Cuz, it's got to be! Yo!"

And then, at exactly the same time, they said "Sheeeet!"

You could cut the tension with a knife. It seemed like an eternity before Rape or Hairy moved. Finally, Rape said, through clenched teeth, "It appears that Mr. Pothead is better studied than I first suspected."

Again, the students looked at each other.

"Does this mean we don't have to do the reading?" Red asked, sheepishly.

"A bargain is a bargain." Rape said, as he turned to leave. He stopped just as he exited, and without turning around and said, "47,000 points deducted from Griffindor for Mr. Pothead being an insufferable know it all."

And with that he exited. The class burst into cheers and applause.

"What the fuck just happened?" Hairy asked.

Chapter Six

"You spoke jive, Hairy." Red answered. "At least, I think it was jive. I've never actually heard it before."

"It was definitely jive" Hornie interjected. "Where did you learn that, Hairy?"

"I don't know." Hairy whispered, "It just sort of came to me. What is jive anyway?"

Hornie answered at once, "It's an archaic street language. No one speaks jive anymore."

"Rape does." Red reminded them. "And evidently so does Hairy."

"What does that mean?" Hairy asked.

"It means there's more to you than meets the eye, Hairy Pothead." Hornie said. "The only other person who can speak jive is...you know...WHO."

Somewhere, an owl hooted.

Sheeet! Hairy thought.

Chapter 7

Brooms

The other students were still yammering about Hairy's showdown with Rape when they went to their next class, Broomsticks, taught by Professor Twig. They met in the courtyard where several brooms lay about on the ground. Learning to fly on a broomstick was one of the most basic things they would learn here at Hawgsleg. In fact, most of them had never been on a broom alone before, as the practice was forbidden by wizarding law until you had been properly trained. Red had explained all of this to Hairy before they got to their first class.

Between Red, Hornie and his occasional conversations with Mostly Bodiless Merl, Hairy had learned a lot of wizard etiquette in just a few days. And if he ever got in trouble, there was always the book. Tucked neatly in Hairy's back pocket, it was his insurance policy if he ever found himself in a really tight spot. At least that's how he thought about it. So far, he hadn't taken a peek. Preferring to live his life as he had before coming to Hawgsleg, by the seat of his pants.

Each student had positioned themselves beside a broom, awaiting Professor Twig's arrival. Drago took the un-chaperoned opportunity to give Hairy a hard time.

"Think you're big shit after what you did to Rape, do you douche bag?" Drago drawled.

"Give it a rest, Drago," Hornie said, hotly.

This really seemed to piss Drago off.

"Does you girlfriend fight all your battles for you, Pothead?" He said.

Crabs and Herpes guffawed stupidly.

"Shut up, dickwad!" Red screamed. It looked as if they might all come to blows, but it was at that point (thank goodness!) that Professor Twig appeared. There was an awkward couple moments of silence.

"Well, don't just stand there. Pick up your brooms and get to it." She commanded.

Brooms

"Ma'am," Red inquired "Most of us have never flown a broom before. Are we going to learn fly today?"

Professor Twig pierced him with a stare, "Of course not. You're going to learn to sweep, you messy little shits!"

Chapter 8

Chasing the Golden Snatch

She hadn't been kidding. Once the entire castle had been swept, mopped and all of the base boards dusted, the students retired to their individual dorms. Hairy and Red were taking tokes off old Betsy, chillin' in their room. Hairy was leaned back on his bed. His first day of school was behind him, and he'd learned a lot...of course, none of it was in the classroom, but what the hell! Education was as much about one's experiences as the lectures they attended or the papers they wrote or the frogs they dissected.

"You going out for any extracurricular's?" Red asked Hairy, looking at a school brochure.

"Like what?" Hairy responded.

"I don't know. There's a lot of stuff. Chess team. Basket weaving. Snatch Chasing. Golf..."

Chasing the Golden Snatch

"Wait," Hairy interrupted. "What did you say?"

"Golf?"

"Before that."

"Basket weaving?"

"After that!"

"Snatch Chasing?"

"Yeah! That!" Hairy said, excitedly. "What's that?"

"You've never chased Snatch before?" Red asked, incredulously.

"Plenty of it," Hairy assured him. "I just didn't know it was a sport."

"Of course it's a sport! In fact, it's the most popular sport in the whole Wizarding World."

"Where do I sign up?" Hairy asked. Red looked at the brochure and jumped up.

"Great gobs of goose shit, Hairy! The meeting is going on right now! If we hurry we can make it!"

They rushed out of their dorm and into the castle proper. They flew down the corridor and made it just in time to the room where the meeting was going to take place. There were several other students who were already there, obviously interested in joining the team too, including a couple of deep-voiced girls with short haircuts (lesbians no doubt).

Professors Twig, Rape, McGanja and Dopey entered and started the meeting and for the sake of the first year students, explained how the game worked. It was probably more for his own sake, Hairy figured, as Capturing the Golden Snatch was, after all, the most popular sport in all of the Wizarding World. Even more popular than soccer, which Hairy hated anyway. If he'd wanted to see a bunch of guys trying to score for 90 minutes, he could go to his local pub.

Evidently the goal of the game was simple. Somewhere on the Hawgsleg campus was a gorgeous blonde. Only one. Hairy hadn't noticed before but sure enough as he scanned the room, the closest thing he found to a blonde was Drago and he could hardly be called a blonde. Hairy was pretty sure he spotted some tiny dark roots amidst all that white hair. In fact, he couldn't think of a single blonde in any of his classes.

The first person to nail the blonde, or "Capture the Golden Snatch", was the winner of the game. It sounded easy to Hairy, but Red assured him it was far more difficult than it sounded. Evidently, the blonde in question was quite fast and slippery and that wasn't all, she was one of those chatterbox types who didn't know when to shut the fuck up. Hairy was determined not to let any of this deter him. He hadn't gotten laid in so long he'd forgotten what a naked woman even looked like. Would he even remember what to do with the Golden Snatch if he were to catch it? He'd better spend some time on the internet catching up on the latest positions and fetishes.

When the meeting ended, Hornie walked into the room, saying, "What's up guys?"

"We just signed up to chase the Golden Snatch," Red told her. "Maybe you'd be interest in signing up for the team, too?"

"Don't be absurd," she replied. "I have no interest in chasing snatch."

"Goddamn it," Hairy said, quietly, and handed Red a ten pound note. Red grinned, and said, under his breath, "Told you so."

"Hornie?" Harry said, "Why are there no blondes at Hawgsleg?"

"That's easy," she answered. "Blondes are stupid."

"Surely not all of them are stupid?" Hairy asked.

Chapter Eight

"I suppose not," she replied, considering.
"The Golden Snatch isn't stupid I suppose, or
she'd never have been accepted to Hawgsleg.
No, I figure that probably 99.9% of blondes
are total airheads, but I haven't done the math
and I won't be doing it anytime soon. I'll be far
too busy with my own club."

"You joined a club?" Red asked, surprised.

"Yes, the homework club."

"Figures," Red scoffed no longer surprised
at all.

"Would you guys want to do homework
with me?" Hornie asked.

"When?" Hairy inquired.

"Right now," she said, as if it was obvious.

Hairy and Red looked at each other,
pleading with their eyes for the other to come
up with an excuse. Hairy shook his head. He
had nothing. They were stuck. Try as they
might neither one of them could think of a
reasonable excuse to get them out of there.

"Let's work on spell casting," Hornie
suggested.

"Great," Hairy groaned. "My absolute worst
subject."

"You think you're bad?" Red said. "I'm the
worst spell caster ever."

Chasing the Golden Snatch

"You are not." Hairy argued.

"Am too."

"Are not."

"AM TOO!"

"Ok! You really are," Hairy conceded, laughing. "You really are terrible."

They all laughed.

"Alright boys, that's enough. Let's get started with the disarming spell," Hornie instructed, pulling out her wand. It was large and purple with an extra attachment shaped like a hummingbird, which made it slightly intimidating. "I've been practicing, so, I'll go first. Both of you, pull out your wands as if you are going to use them on me."

Hairy and Red looked at each other and shrugged. Hairy pulled his big black wand out of his pocket.

"Nice wand, Hairy!" Hornie said, appreciatively. "A goodly length and circumference. But do you know how to use it?"

In truth, Hairy suspected that he did not, and that Hornie could teach him a thing or two about the subject. Red drew his wand. It was small. Tiny in fact. Hairy and Hornie couldn't stop staring at it.

"What?" Red asked, clueless.

"Your wand..." Hairy began and stopped.

"...It's so small," Hornie finished for him.

"It's a hand me down," Red said, defensively. "Besides, Professor Dopey says it isn't the size of the wand, but the ability of the wand wielder."

Now Hairy and Hornie looked at each other, finally, unable to contain themselves they laughed out loud, "BWAH-HA-HA-HA-HA!!!"

"Can we get on with this?" Red huffed.

"Sure thing," Hornie said, trying to contain her laughter. "Now, raise your wands as if you were about to attack me with them."

They held up their wands. The difference in Hairy's and Red's wands was so dramatic, that Hornie and Hairy dissolved again into laughter.

Red's face changed color to match his hair and through gritted teeth announced, "I'm going to dinner. This is a complete waste of time."

"No," Hornie grabbed his arm. "I'm sorry, Red. I'll refrain from laughing. I promise."

Red and Hairy returned to their positions and raised their wands. Together they stepped toward her.

Chasing the Golden Snatch

"DROPDATIUS!" Hornie shouted, pointing her wand at Red, and with that his itsy-bitsy wand flew from his hand.

"DROPDATIUS!" She repeated, turning to Hairy and his wand likewise flew through the air and landed several feet from them.

"Excellent, Hornie!" Hairy said.

"Good show!" Red added.

"Thank you!" Hornie said, proudly. "Pretty soon I'll be good enough to disarm two opponents with one spell."

"I want to try next," Red said, retrieving Hornie and Hairy's wands.

Returning to their original spots, Hairy asked, "Are you sure you want to do this, Red?"

"Practice makes perfect," Red replied. So Hairy and Hornie lifted their wands. Red did the same.

"Are you ready?" Hairy asked.

"Ready." Red answered.

They made a move towards him.

"DROPDATIUS." Red yelled, but instead of disarming the two of them, Red's trousers dropped to his ankles, exposing lacey, pink women's panties underneath. Hairy and Hornie were unable to stop their momentum and the three of them toppled over into a tangled heap, a flailing pile of arms and legs. Just at that moment, Drago, Crabs and Herpes walked by, and seeing them, laughed loudly.

"See guys," Drago sneered, "What did I tell you? A bunch of freaks!"

Hairy, Hornie and Red righted themselves. Red muttering, while pulling up his pants, "I guess I need more practice."

"I agree." Hairy said, smiling.

"What are you idiots doing?" Drago asked.

"None of your fucking business," Red spat.

"Oh yeah, Pinky?" Drago said, pulling out his long, silver, metallic-looking wand and pointing it straight at Red. "Looks like you were practicing spell casting to me."

"Leave him alone, Drago." Hornie said.

"Or what?" Drago replied, sneering at her. They stared at each other a moment. Suddenly, Drago shouted, "SUMNABITCHIUS!"

A bolt of orange energy shot from the tip of his wand and hit Red straight on the mouth.

"MOTHERFUCKINGGODDAMNSON OFABITCHBASTARDFUCKINGSHITASS HOLEHELLGODDAMNFUCKFUCKFUCK

Chasing the Golden Snatch

FUCKFUCKFUCKFUCKFUCKFUCK!!!"
Red screamed, and repeated ad nauseam,
unable to stop cussing.

"Oh no!" Hairy said. "It's the cursing curse!
Red won't be able to stop cursing for 24
hours!"

"How could you?" Hornie accused Drago.

"Teach him to run his mouth to me!" Drago
retorted.

"You had better run," Hornie said, with a
sadistic look in her eye. The three of them
didn't move. She raised her wand and shouted,
"ASSYHOLEO!"

A brown bolt of energy shot out of her
wand and hit Drago, Crabs and Herpes right in
their asses. There was a large gurgling sound as
the three perpetrators looked at one another and
grabbed their bottoms.

"OH SHIT!" Drago shrieked, as a great
farting noise culminated from the three of
them. They ran out of the room as fast as they
could, though unfortunately, not fast enough.

"Was that what I think it was?" Hairy
asked, tentatively.

"Yes," Hornie answered. "the Diarrhea
Curse. They'll have a violent and aggressive
set of the runs for the next week and a half."

Chapter Eight

"Remind me not to piss you off," Hairy
said, with a shiver. "Ever."

"Shall we go to dinner now?" Hornie asked.

"Let's" Hairy agreed. "What do you say,
Red?

"MOTHERFUCKINGGODDAMNSONOF
ABITCHBASTARDFUCKINGSHITHELL
ASSHOLEGODDAMNFUCKFUCKFUCK
FUCKFUCKFUCKFUCKFUCKFUCK!!!"
Red replied, but that was good enough for
them. So they left for the dining room not
noticing an absolutely gorgeous blonde who
passed them in the corridor on the way down.

Chapter 9

Hairy's Best Ho Ever

Between classes, dodging Drago and his goons, and chasing the Golden Snatch, the first half of the school year passed pretty quickly, with Hairy never once reading a single page from the book in his pocket. Then, the days got colder and it was time for Christmas break. Hairy had never really had much of a Christmas with the Doofuses. The thought of watching his cousin open his presents just didn't fill Hairy with much Christmas spirit, so he decided to remain at Hawgsleg for the duration of the holiday. He'd eat better here and he could explore the castle more, something he dearly loved to do. Especially if he found a little corner to hide away and toke up. It was almost like a game to him.

Chapter Nine

Red was going to be staying as well. His parents were going to be in Amsterdam, where they vacationed every year, so he thought it'd be more fun to hang out and get high with Hairy, and who knew, maybe the Golden Snatch would be staying over the holidays as well. It seemed like a long shot, but what the hell?

Hornie, on the other hand was going home for Christmas. Her parents were taking a big trip across the pond to the States, to a magical place called Colorado. They claimed it was for the great skiing, but Hornie said it was because pot was legal there.

As Christmas Eve approached, Hairy felt a little restless. He went to bed that night thinking about his parents and all the Christmases they had missed spending together. He did think about them often, but holidays were the worst. Especially Christmas.

"WAKE UP HAIRY!" a loud voice said in his ear. "HAIRY! PRESENTS!"

Hairy opened his eyes with some effort. Red was right there in his face, his breath reeking.

"What?" Harry said, confused.

"Let's open presents!" Red insisted.

"I got presents?"

"Of course you did silly, it's Christmas!"

The two of them ran down to the main hall where the Christmas tree was located. The few other students who'd stay over the holiday were there, also opening presents. Some were from their relatives, but some were from Santa Claus, Hairy noted. The only people not opening presents were the Sneaky Snakes who were all on someone's naughty list, obviously.

"This is from my mother," Red said, handing Hairy a decent sized package.

"What do you think it is?" Hairy asked.

"Oh, I know what it is." Red replied. "I'm sure I got one too. She makes me a new one every year."

Hairy couldn't wait. He tore into the package to find a crazy multi-colored blazer. He was overwhelmed with feelings of elation at having received a present and awestruck at the sheer ridiculousness of the gift itself. He tried to vocalize his gratitude, "It's....it's...."

Red nodded, "Ridiculous. I know. But she means well. She calls it my coat of many colors. Like in the Dolly Parton song."

"Dolly Parton?" Hairy asked.

Chapter Nine

"She's a big fan," Red said, rolling his eyes. "BIG FAN. See? I got one too. I get a new one every year. She even made one for Hornie." He held up an unopened package that had Hornie's name on it. They both put their jackets on.

"Bloody hell!" Red exclaimed. "We look like used car salesmen!"

"We do, sort of," Hairy agreed.

"Look." Red said, pointing at another package under the tree. It had Hairy's name on it and said it was from Santa.

"Wonder who that's from?" Hairy mused.

"It says it's from Santa," Red observed.

"But I don't even believe in Santa." Hairy said.

The room went quiet.

"Don't believe in Santa?" Red asked. "That's ridiculous. What kind of wizard are you?"

"The kind of wizard that doesn't believe in Santa Claus, I guess," Hairy said, shrugging. "Are you telling me you do?"

"Of course," Red said. "Santa's a wizard too. He attended Hawgsleg himself, a long time ago."

"Are you putting me on?" Hairy asked.

"No," Red insisted. "He was in Merv Griffindor house, just like us."

Hairy did not believe a word of it until Red produced a very old year book with Santa's picture in it. *Son of a bitch.* Hairy thought. How come the fat bastard never brought him any presents when he was growing up at the Doofuses? If he ever saw Santa in person maybe he'd ask him that question.

"Are you going to open your present?" Red asked. In all the hubbub debating the existence of Santa, Hairy had completely forgotten the very thing that had triggered the argument in the first place. He opened the package and found...a cape.

It was unlike anything Hairy had ever seen. The fabric itself seemed to be water and cloth all at the same time. It flowed over his hands, smooth as silk. He couldn't even tell what color it was because it seemed to reflect and absorb all the colors in the room. He almost didn't believe that it could exist and yet it was right there in front of him.

"It's a cape," he said.

"A cape?" Red asked. "Like a Batman cape? Is there a mask too?"

Chapter Nine

"No mask," Hairy said, looking inside the box. "But there is a note." He took it out and read it.

> This once belonged to your father.
> It's yours now to use as you see fit.
> Stay out of trouble.
> Ho, ho, ho.

Great. Hairy thought. *My very first gift from Santa is something that had been re-gifted.* But then he thought about his long lost father. He hadn't a single possession of his dad's, except for his last name. He pulled the cape out of the box and threw it over his shoulders.

"How do I look?" Hairy asked.

"What?" Red returned.

"In the cape. Do I look like a vampire? Like Rob Pattinson?"

"What are you talking about? Who's Rob Pattinson?"

"How do I look in the bloody cape?" Hairy asked again, somewhat annoyed that Red was playing a game with him.

"What in the holy hell are you going on about?"

"The cape!" Hairy said, taking it off. "How did it look?

"What?" Red said. "Put it on and let me see."

"I just did," Hairy insisted.

"No, you didn't." Red said.

"Have you smoked yourself daft?"

"Probably," Red snorted. "But I still don't know what you're talking about."

"Maybe the cape's magical." Hairy pondered. "I'm going to put it back on. Tell me what you see."

"Ok." Red said.

"Ready?" Hairy asked.

"Yep."

Hairy slipped the cape back on.

"What do you see?" Hairy asked.

"What?" Red said.

"Do you see me?"

"I guess?"

"What do you mean 'I guess'? You either see me or you don't!"

"I see you."

"What about the cape?"

"What cape?"

"The cape I'm wearing. The one Santa gave to me!" Hairy fairly shouted.

Chapter Nine

"I have no idea what you're talking about!" Ron shouted back.

Hairy took the cape off.

"Did you do it?" Ron asked. "Did you put the cape on?"

"Yes."

"I don't remember you having it on." Ron said, looking confused.

"Maybe I was invisible...but I don't think so, because you were talking to me."

"Wait," Red ran out of the room and returned with a book. "I think I know what this is."

He flipped through the book and stopped on a page, gasped and exclaimed, "Cor Blimey! That is a Cloak of Incredulity."

"Cloak of Incredulity? What's that?" Hairy asked.

"It has the ability to shroud the wearer in a state of confusion such that all who view the wearer will be overcome with an unwillingness to believe what they see or hear," Red read aloud.

"That sounds incredibly convoluted." Hairy commented.

"It's bloody brilliant!" Red said, excitedly. "It's just as good as being invisible! Hold on, there's more." He continued reading. "It's an extremely rare magical artifact, whose origin and whereabouts are unknown."

"Is it the only one of its kind?" Hairy asked.

"Sounds like it, doesn't it?" Red replied.

"Then how in the hell did my father get his hands on it?" Hairy wondered.

"The answer is obvious," Red said. "Santa Claus."

Hairy wasn't convinced and he wasn't even looking at the cloak.

"Think of all the shit we can do with this cloak," Red said, obviously imagining all the possibilities.

"The note said specifically to stay out of trouble." Hairy reminded him.

"It also said it was yours to use as you see fit."

Red was right. It did say that. They racked their pot addled brains and decided the very best use for the cloak was to sneak into the women's showers!

It had been Hairy's best Christmas ever and that night, after the celebration with punch and cake, as he lay in bed, almost asleep, he heard a familiar noise.

"Gobble-gobble-gobble."

Chapter Nine

What the hell? Hairy thought. He and Red both arose, looking at each other. The noise was coming from under Hairy's bed.

"Is that who I think it is?" Red asked.

Hairy bent over and looked under his bed and indeed, it was his old pal, Butterball.

"What are you doing under there?" Hairy asked.

"What the hell does it look like I'm doing? I'm hiding."

"From who?"

"Who do you think?" Butterball smarted off. "The damn Chef!"

"Chef Cliché?" Red asked.

"Yes," Butterball said, "The French Chef, Chef Cliché."

"Would you come out from under there?" Hairy requested. Butterball crawled out from under the bed and sat on it beside Hairy.

"Where have you been?" Hairy asked, "I haven't seen you in forever."

"I've been keeping it on the down low for a while," Butterball said. "This is turkey eating season, you know. Besides, it ain't like you get any mail anyway, Hairy. I get pretty bored hanging around with the other turkeys here."

Hairy thought for a minute.

"Butterball, what if there was a way for you to hide out in plain sight?"

"Huh?" the turkey said.

Hairy explained to Butterball about the Cloak of Incredulity and offered to let her use it during the day while he and the others were in class. At night, she could hang out under his bed all she wanted. That way they could still use it to explore. Butterball loved the idea, and the three of them got high and drifted off to dreamland that Christmas Eve, with Hairy dreaming of fat blunts, full hookahs and naked blondes.

Chapter 10

Puff

Christmas had passed and school had resumed. Hairy and Red had indeed tried to use the cloak for nefarious purposes such as sneaking into the women's showers. However, they had been foiled at every attempt by the cock blocking ghost of Fertile Myrtle, who always warned the girls in the shower that she felt the presence of boys nearby. Evidently, the cloak couldn't conceal them entirely from the ghost. Bitch.

When Hornie returned to school they had let her in on their little secret, and the three of them had gone on numerous adventures, exploring the castle, and getting high in places they shouldn't. Like the roof, Dumbass' office,

and Rape's torture chamber in the dungeon.
(Now that was a truly scary place.)

As promised, they would let Butterball use
the cloak while they were in class. Apparently,
she was still being hunted by Chef Cliché, who
had found a wonderful new recipe for roast
Turkey alamode. They weren't prepared for
what happened one evening however, when
Butterball came running into the Main Hall
where they were all studying.

"Help! Help me!" Butterball screamed.

"Is Chef Cliché after you again,
Butterball?" Red asked, but Butterball didn't
have enough time to answer as Groovius
entered carrying a large burlap sack.

"Groovius?" Hairy called to him. "What are
you doing?"

"Yeah," Hornie chimed in. "Why are you
chasing Butterball?"

"We were playing tag?" Groovius said,
unsure.

"Bullshit!" Butterball shrieked. "You were
trying to put me in that big ass sack!"

"What?" Groovius said. "This here sack?"

"Yeah," Butterball said. "That sack.

"Would you believe I was playing sack
tag?"

"Not for a fucking minute," Hairy said.

"Ok, ok, you got me, Hairy," Groovius said. "I need that there bird."

"For what?"

"Dinner."

At that word, Butterball fainted.

"She fainted," Ron stated.

"You can't eat Butterball, Groovius," Hornie explained. "She's our friend."

"I wasn't going to eat her myself." Groovius replied.

"Then who was going to eat her?"

"I can't say, Hornie."

"Why not?" Hornie asked.

"The walls have ears. It ain't safe. I can show you though, if you want. Later. Down at my cottage. Come see me, but don't let anyone else see you come. You guys got that?" Groovius said all this in a whisper with his eyes shifting around to rest on the other occupants of the room. They agreed to go later, after everyone had gone to sleep. That was when they usually used the cloak to sneak around the castle anyway. Groovius left them to return to his cottage.

"Imagine that?" Hornie said. "Groovius wanting to serve up Butterball!"

Puff

"He must have had his reasons, Hornie," Hairy reassured her. " Groovius is a pretty practical guy. Still, it is a pretty shady way to treat a friend." Then after a pause. "Say, you guys wanna get high?"

"Damn straight," Hornie said, and they all left to get their smoking paraphernalia, leaving poor Butterball sprawled out on the floor and not noticing Drago, who was hiding around the corner listening to every word.

Around midnight, they threw the cloak over their collective shoulders and sneaked out of the castle. Hairy had noticed a strange thing about the cloak. It seemed to accommodate whatever person or persons were underneath it. Be it their turkey friend, or the three of them. He wondered what limitations it had. Could he fit a car under it for example? Or a half acre of pot perhaps. That would deter John Law from messing with his crop, wouldn't it?

Groovius' cottage was located down the hill from the castle proper. They made it to the front door and knocked. The door opened and there stood Groovius, wearing a purple silk bath robe with big furry, bunny slippers. A shower cap covered his afro.

Chapter Ten

"Come on in, cats." He ushered them across the threshold. Groovius' cottage was delightfully decorated. In fact, Hairy thought to himself, it was nothing at all like he'd envisioned. It was neither rustic nor decorated with any ethnic sensibility. It was almost feminine, with its lace curtains and pink doilies.

"Ok," Hornie began. "Why are we here, Groovius? What is it you want to show us?"

"This," he said, and he whistled. From the bedroom came a dragon, nearly human sized. It ran right up to Groovius and started nuzzling him and licking his face.

"Is that what I think it is?" Hairy asked, intimidated a bit. "Is that a..."

"A dragon," Hornie confirmed.

"Bloody brilliant," Red said. "Where'd you get that?"

"I know a guy," Groovius hedged. They'd known Groovius long enough to know he'd probably procured the dragon through illegal means. He really was a walking stereotype in this fashion.

"I call him Puff," Groovius said.

"Like that old song?" Hornie asked.

"What song?" Groovius said.

Puff

"Never mind," she said.

"Nah, I call him Puff for other reasons." Groovius said. "Watch this. Puff, fetch for daddy, would you?"

With that, Puff ran enthusiastically into the other room, returning with an enormous (and I mean, ENORMOUS!) bong.

"Shall we smoke?" Groovius asked them with a smile. And so they did. Like crazy. But the craziest thing of all was how much the dragon smoked. He'd take in a great puff from the bong and blow it all over the cottage. Talk about a contact high! It was one of the most pleasant things Hairy had ever been a part of.

"Got any Funyuns, Groovius?" Hairy asked.

"Hell yeah, I got Funyuns," Groovius said. "Puff, get us some Funyuns."

Puff got up out of his chair and went to the pantry, but all he found were empty Funyun bags, which he brought back to Groovius.

"What?" he said. "Out of Funyuns?" Puff nodded yes. "Then we'll have to go get some more."

"Dude," Red said, "It's like 2 AM! Everything's closed."

"Shit," Groovius said. "You're right."

"Nuh uh," Hornie said. "The gas station is open and they got Funyuns for sale."

They all agreed that going to the gas station was the only option that made any sense. The problem? All of them were too fucked up to drive.

"I've got an idea," Groovius said. "I'll send Puff. He's a dragon. He doesn't have to drive, he can fly."

"Bloody brilliant," Red said, apparently this was becoming his catch phrase.

"Wait!" Hairy interrupted. "Won't the clerk at the gas station freak out when they see a dragon...buying Funyuns?"

"Shit." Groovius said. "You're right, Hairy. You're always right."

"Wait a minute," Hornie said. "What if we disguise him as a person?"

"Yeah," Groovius said. "You're right. You're always right."

So, they dressed Puff in one of Groovius' hats and coats. Groovius handed Puff a ten pound note and said, "You bring me back the change now, you hear?"

Puff opened the door to leave, only to be met by Drago, who'd been peeping through the keyhole. Drago screamed. Puff screamed.

Puff

Everyone screamed. Alas, it was not for ice cream.

Only fifteen minutes had passed, but to Hairy it seemed like a lifetime. Only a few minutes ago they had been sitting in Groovius' cottage smoking the enormous bong and figuring out how to get some Funyuns. Now, they were all sitting in Dumbass' office, waiting for him to arrive.

He was seated directly in front of Dumbass' desk with Red on his right and Hornie on his left. To her left sat Drago. They could hear Dumbass and McGanja talking just outside the door, so none of them spoke a word.

It was then that something caught Hairy's eye. Sitting right there on Dumbass' desk was a great big bowl of peanuts. Hairy pointed to them, and then to his stomach. He had the munchies. Bad. They all did. Hornie shook her head "no" at Hairy, who turned to see what Red thought. Red nodded yes and pointed at his own stomach. It was like having an angel on one shoulder and a devil on the other. Hairy turned toward the door, and hearing that the conversation was continuing, reached over to the bowl of peanuts and grabbed a handful,

Chapter Ten

tossing half of them in his own mouth and giving the rest to Red, who did likewise.

Drago's jaw dropped hard. He could not believe the audacity of Hairy Pothead. Hairy just grinned at him, which only upset Drago that much more. Red snickered out loud, then caught himself. Hairy reached over and grabbed another handful of nuts. This time he offered Hornie first dibs. This time she didn't resist, and took half of the handful Hairy had pilfered. He gave the rest to Red and grabbed another handful out of the bowl. This handful he offered to Drago who shook his head no aggressively. Hairy and crew finished off the bowl, licking their fingers when they were all gone. It was at that point, Dumbass and McGanja entered.

"Thank you for your patience, students." Dumbass said, sitting at his desk. Professor McGanja stood beside him to his left.

"This is serious..." Dumbass began, but then noticed that his peanut bowl was empty.

"Curious," he murmured looking around, as if he'd misplaced them. "Hmmmm... well as I was saying, this business with the dragon is quite serious, as any business with dragons is wont to be."

Puff

"What's going to happen to Puff?" Hornie asked. "He's such a friendly dragon."

"Yes, he is quite friendly, Ms. Stranger, you are quite right about that. We'll find a proper home for Puff, don't you worry about that."

"And what about Groovius?" Red squeaked.

"Groovius Haggard will also be dealt with appropriately." Dumbass said.

"Wonderful, sir," Hairy said. "Now, if that's all we'll just get out of here and let you work."

"Very good," Dumbass said, and Hairy started to rise.

"Not so fast, Mr. Pothead." McGanja interjected, and Hairy sat back down. "You aren't getting off that easy." She gave a severe look to Dumbass, who suddenly recalled what was going on.

"Oh! Yes, that's right. There is still the matter of you sneaking out of the castle past curfew."

"Dumbass," Hairy said.

"Excuse me?" Dumbass intoned, a hint of danger underneath the calm.

"Professor Dumbass...with all due respect, we're thirty years old, is it fair to impose such a strict curfew on us?"

Chapter Ten

Dumbass sat back in his chair and stroked his long white beard.

"It's true, that curfew was set with the intention that our students would be between the ages of eleven and seventeen. However, as it is the rule on the books, it is still the rule and rules cannot be ignored even if they are dumb."

Hairy didn't like where this seemed to be heading.

"When rules are broken," Dumbass continued, "Then there must be punishment. And as Headmaster, it is my job to mete out an appropriate punishment that fits the breaking of this dumb rule. Therefore I will issue a detention to you and your friends."

Detention? Hairy thought. Maybe this wouldn't be so bad.

"You will spend your detention in the Forest of No Return."

"WTF?" Hairy thought...evidently out loud, as evidence by the quotation marks, he continued quietly, "Sorry."

"Allow me to finish," Dumbass said. "I need you and your friends to search for a unicorn in the forest, Hairy. Do you think you can do that?"

"Yes, sir," Hairy said.

"Good."

"Wait a minute!" Drago interrupted, jumping out of his chair. "This doesn't sound like a punishment to me."

"Mr. Malfeasance? I did say their detention was in the Forest of No Return, did I not?"

"Yeah, that part's actually pretty cool," Drago said. "I just thought there'd be more you know...MORE."

"Perhaps Mr. Malfeasance has a point." Dumbass considered it.

"Git," Red said.

"Shit," Hairy said.

ASSYHOLEO, Hornie mouthed. Drago grabbed his ass and sat down, fast.

"Under the circumstances, a deduction of house points seems appropriate I think, don't you, Professor McGanja?"

"If you say so." She answered.

"5 points deducted from each of you for breaking curfew. Does that sound appropriate, Professor McGanja?"

"If you say so." She answered.

"You and your friends should report to detention now, Mr. Pothead."

"Now?" Hairy asked, incredulous.

"Right now," Dumbass insisted.

Chapter Ten

They all got up to leave.

"Please remain, Mr. Malfeasance."

Hairy, Red and Hornie exited the office.

"5 points Professor?" Drago said. "That seems kind of weak to me."

"You think so?" Dumbass asked.

"Yes, I do."

"Mr. Malfeasance, what does it say on my door?"

"I don't know what that has..." Drago began.

"WHAT DOES IT SAY ON MY DOOR, DRAGO?" Dumbass yelled.

"Headmaster," He said sheepishly.

"What? I can't hear you."

"Headmaster, sir."

"You're goddamn right it says Headmaster, you little shit! That means I'll decide what punishments are appropriate or not and you'll learn to live with it. Got that?"

"Yes, sir."

"Louder!"

"YES, SIR" Drago shouted at the top of his voice. "May I go now, sir?"

"Yes." Dumbass said. "You may go with the rest to the Forest of No Return."

"But..." Drago began.

"No buts, Mr. Malfeasance."

"Yes sir."

Drago turned to go.

"Oh, and Mr. Malfeasance…"

"Yes sir?"

"A bazillion points from Sneaky Snake House. How does that sound?"

"Appropriate, sir."

"That's right. Perfectly appropriate. Now get your ass out of my fucking office."

As he got to the door, Drago turned suddenly and said, "They ate all your peanuts, you know."

And with that he was gone. They could hear him sobbing all the way down the hall. Dumbass sat looking at his empty peanut bowl and said, "So, that's where they went. For a moment there, I thought I was going crazy."

"I didn't even know you liked peanuts, Bumble," McGanja remarked.

"I don't, Minnie," Dumbass replied. "I just suck all the chocolate off and put them back in the bowl."

Chapter 11

Shit Gets Real

They stood waiting at the edge of the forest. Why had Dumbass assigned them to do detention here and now, at three in the morning? *Maybe he's just a sadistic motherfucker*, Hairy thought.

The four of them stood there for what seemed like forever. Hairy had brought the cloak with him and decided to put it on. Red and Hornie huddled under it with him. Drago just shivered.

"Is everyone ready?" A voice came from the forest. It belonged to a large shadowy figure that stepped out from behind the trees. It was Groovius. Hornie ran to him and gave him a hug, saying, "Oh Groovius. We thought you were being sacked."

"Sacked?" He said. "Me? Never. Professor Dumbass knows how I like to bring strays home. This isn't the first time I've done this."

Shit Gets Real

"But Groovius, a dragon?"

"Not my first time, I'm telling you."

"What are they going to do with Puff?" Red wondered.

"Dumbass will think of something," Groovius replied. "Always have faith in Bumbling Dumbass. Always."

"What are we doing here, Groovius?" Hairy asked. "And at this hour?"

"Catching a cold," Drago sniffed. They ignored him.

"Something's going on in the forest," Groovius said. "Something real bad."

"And it has something to do with a unicorn?" Hairy asked.

"Yes. Unicorns are some of the most magical creatures on Earth. But the one that lives in the forest hasn't been seen for a couple of days. Dumbass wants us to find it and protect it from harm. We just need our guide to help us to find our way."

"I'm here," Came another voice from behind Groovius. The five of them turned back towards the forest to see a small, furry, creature step from the shadows. It looked like a rabbit of some sort, except for the large set of antlers on its head.

Chapter Eleven

"Jack!" Groovius said, and he and the...whatever the hell it was, embraced. "I want to introduce you guys to my old friend, Jack."

"Pleased to make your acquaintance," Jack said.

"Jack's a Jackalope," Groovius explained and he continued, "He's one of the Guardians of this forest, and a dear old friend of mine. Jack, this is Hornie Stranger, Red Measley, Drago Malfeasance and this is Hairy Pothead."

"THE Hairy Pothead? I'm pleased to meet you, sir," He shook Hairy's hand profusely, completely ignoring the others, who'd been in this position before.

"How do we find the unicorn?" Hairy asked.

"We'll take the path through the forest," Jack told them. "Straying from it would be extremely dangerous. They don't call this the Forest of No Return for no reason."

And so they entered the forest. They illuminated their wands with the Gimmesumgoddamnlightus Spell, and Jack took the lead followed by Hairy, Hornie, Red, Drago and Groovius bringing up the rear. The forest was alive and quite terrifying. They seemed to be surrounded by glowing eyes and low growling noises. More than once, Drago thought he was going to piss himself. They walked and walked,

Shit Gets Real

and the forest only got thicker and darker as they did. Finally, up ahead, Hairy could make out an opening. Suddenly, Jack stopped and signaled for them to do the same. They turned off their wands with the Lightgodafuggaawayus spell. It took a moment for their eyes to adjust to the darkness. The forest was so thick, that the light of the moon could hardly penetrate the dense foliage. They could, however, see two figures illuminated in the clearing ahead. They crept closer and hid behind several large trees. Sure enough, there was the unicorn. Pristine white, glowing and magnificent. The other figure was cloaked. It walked around the unicorn, rubbing it. Stroking it. Talking to it, though they could not make out any of the words.

The figure circled the unicorn a couple times, and then shockingly, pulled a stool up behind the glorious animal and stood on it, dropping his trousers.

"OMG!" Hornie started to say but before she could really blurt it out, Hairy clapped his hand over her mouth. Whoever the shadowy figure was, he was humping the unicorn.

Jack had seen all he could stand. He stepped into the clearing and yelled, "STOP THAT RIGHT NOW, YOU PERV!"

Chapter Eleven

At the sudden noise, the unicorn bolted off back into the forest, leaving the cloaked figure behind.

"You should be ashamed of yourself, Carl!" Jack yelled after the unicorn in a very accusing tone.

"Carl?" Hairy, Red, Hornie and Drago said simultaneously. The shadowy figure drew his wand.

"DIEMUDDAFUGGIO!!!" He screamed as a red bolt of energy just missed Jack, hitting a tree.

"That's the killing curse!" Hornie yelled. "It's one of the forbidden curses! In fact, it's THE forbidden curse. The worst one of all!" They all took cover behind trees, and every one of them was thinking the same thing at the same time, without a single act of magic being performed. *THIS SHIT JUST GOT REAL!*

"Come out and play, Hairy Pothead," the shadowy figure said in a voice that was curiously familiar.

"Yes," another voice said in a hiss, but it had also seemed to come from the same shadowy figure.

"It's all come full circle, hasn't it, Pothead?" the hissing voice said.

"Grabuspaulbunyonus!" The other voice cried and a green bold of energy spread out from the dark figure all over the trees. Suddenly, the trees came alive and they reached down and ensnared the group. Everyone that is except for Hairy. He was still wearing the Cloak! It must be protecting him somehow! He tried to pull the branches free from the friends, but he wasn't strong enough. Even their mouths were covered by the branches, probably to keep them from casting any spells.

"DROPDATIUS!" Hairy yelled, trying the disarming spell, but it didn't work against the tree branches.

"Come out from behind that tree, Hairy Pothead." It was the first voice again, and Hairy didn't see as he had any choice. So he did what the voice had asked him to do and found himself face to face with...

"Professor Squirrel?" Hairy asked.

"Uh, yes, Hairy. Good old Professor Squirrel."

"Why are you doing this, Professor?"

"What do you mean, Hairy?" Squirrel said, confused.

"Oh, Hairy. Poor addle-brained Hairy Pothead," The other voice said. "Haven't you figured any of this out yet?"

"Not really," Hairy admitted. "Why were you humping that unicorn?"

Chapter Eleven

"Unicorns are extremely magical," the voice said. "Humping one, as you call it, can make you immortal, Hairy. You should try it."

"Gross!" Hairy gagged. "That unicorn was a dude!"

"Let me see him," the voice hissed.

"Who is that?" Hairy asked.

"Yes!" Said the voice. "WHO!"

An owl hooted, soon to be joined by another and another and another, until it sounded like an army of owls.

"Where is that voice coming from?" Hairy queried, looking around the clearing.

"Show him," the voice hissed, louder. "Show him my face. Show him WHO I am!"

Squirrel turned around with his back to Hairy, unraveling his turban, as he did, Hairy could make out a face...a face on the back of Squirrel's head, a face...wearing a mask. With horned ears and large round eyes and feathers. An owl mask.

IT WAS KING OWL JR.! The Owl King. The one who'd killed Hairy's parents and left him with a pot leaf scar on his forehead.

"I presume you know WHO I am?" King Owl Jr. said.

"I do," Hairy replied.

"And you know why we're here, Hairy?"

Shit Gets Real

"Not at all."

"I'm going to kill you, Hairy. Once and for all."

"Why? What did I ever do to you?" Hairy wondered, incredulous.

"You made me, Hairy."

"I made you?"

"Yes."

"Bullshit."

"No Hairy, it's true. You made me and I made you."

"That's just weird." Hairy mused.

"We're connected, Hairy. You and I. Forever, and the only way to free myself of you is to kill you off." King Owl Jr. announced.

"You will NEVER be able to kill me off. I know your secret, Owl King."

"What are you talking about Pothead?"

At that, Hairy reached over and pulled the owl mask off. Revealing a fairly attractive older woman."

"What have you done?" She hissed. "I'll kill you for this!"

"I don't think so King Owl Jr." He said. "Or should I say, JK ROWLING!!!"

She screamed and the trees trembled at her wrath, "I'll kill you off for this! I'll kill off everyone you know! Your family! Your friends! Your pets!"

"Oh yeah?" Hairy said, "You need to understand something, Ms. Rowling. My life is my own now and I'll be writing the sequel." He pulled the book out of his back pocket that had been there all year…that is, except for one hour tonight, when he'd taken it out to read the final chapter. He tossed it to JK Rowling, who caught it and just stared at it.

"No, Hairy. You can't do this to me," she pleaded.

Hairy pulled out his wand in a swift motion, and murmured…

"Diemuddafuggio."

A green bolt of energy shot out of his wand, instantly killing Squirrel and JK Rowling as well. The owls stopped hooting. Hairy stood over their two-faced lifeless body. He kicked it. Evidently, their deaths caused the spell on the trees to be broken as his friends joined him in the clearing.

"Hairy?" Hornie said. "Are you ok?"

"Yep!" He said, smiling at her.

"I can't believe it. You used the Killing Curse."

"Yep."

Shit Gets Real

"You killed them Hairy. Squirrel. Rowling. The Owl King."

"Looks like it."

"I...I just can't believe it."

"Why not? They were going to kill me. Why wouldn't I use the Killing Curse?"

"It's unforgiveable," Hornie said.

"For who?" Hairy said.

They turned to Groovius, he put his hands up in defense and shook his head, "Don't look at me. I'm actually a wizard school dropout."

Chapter 12

Setting Up the Sequel

Hairy, Red and Hornie stood in the Main Hall. It had been a couple weeks since they had faced off against Squirrel and King Owl JR.

"What a crazy first year," Red said.

"Yes. If our entire time at Hawgsleg is anything like this past year, it's going to be a real adventure," Hornie observed.

"Oh," Hairy said, "I have a feeling our adventures are going to get much longer and more adult oriented."

"Why do you say that, Hairy?" Hornie asked. "Been reading ahead have you?"

But something had caught Hairy's eyes.

"I'll be right back," He said and he ran off.

"What's his deal?" Hornie asked.

"I'm not sure," Red answered as Dumbass entered the hall.

Setting up the Sequel

"Everyone heading home for the summer?" Dumbass asked the students.

"Yes, sir, Professor Dumbass," Hornie said, adding. "Professor? May I ask a question?"

"Of course Ms. Stranger. Ask me anything."

"What is to become of Puff?" She said.

"Why, we have found the perfect place for our friendly dragon, Ms. Stranger. He will become the new mascot of the fourth Hawgsleg House. The one that used to have the bird. Henceforth, they will be known as the Puffs."

"Isn't that awfully similar to the Huff N' Puff House name?" She asked.

"Ms. Stranger, do you know what it says on my door?"

"I do," She answered.

"If I want to call them the Puffs, "he said in a soft, friendly, yet terrifying tone. "Or the Dingleberrydumbasses, that's exactly what we'll call them."

"Yes, sir," She said.

"And where has Mr. Pothead gotten off to?" Dumbass asked.

"I don't know," Red said. "He was just here a couple minutes ago."

Chapter Twelve

Hairy entered, zipping up his trousers as he did. He smiled and said, "I've done it! I've captured the Golden Snatch!"

At that, a beautiful blonde entered. She kissed Hairy passionately and exited.

"You weren't gone but a few minutes, Hairy!" Hornie said.

"Ok. You've got me," Hairy said. "I captured her twice."

"It seems you have, Hairy," Dumbass said, "But unfortunately, the school year is over, I can't award you any points for your victory."

"Too bad," Red said. "I guess the Sneaky Snakes will win the house cup then."

"WHAT???" Dumbass exclaimed. "How can this be?"

"We were only a couple points behind them in the standings," Red said. "It's a shame really. Rules are rules though."

"Rules are rules, Mr. Measley," Dumbass said, "Unless you are the Headmaster of Hawgsleg. And what does it say on my door?"

"Headmaster?" Red said.

"LOUDER!" Dumbass said.

"HEADMASTER!" Red, Hornie, and Hairy yelled in unison.

Setting up the Sequel

"Goddamn straight!" Dumbass said. "A gazillion points to Merv Griffindor House!"

They all applauded and cheered.

"Professor Dumbass?" Hairy asked, as they headed for the door. "Have we seen the last of the Owl King?"

"You tell me." Dumbass said. "You are writing this story now."

Hairy thought about it a moment.

"What can you tell me about this chamber pot that's hidden somewhere here on campus."

"A chamber pot?" Red asked. "What's that?"

"It's something you piss in, Red," Hornie said.

"Yes, indeed," Dumbass continued. "And this particular chamber pot is supposed to contain many, many secrets I'm told."

Hairy had a thought. He'd smoked weed with nearly everyone here at Hawgsleg, except the Headmaster himself. Should he ask him?

"Professor?" He said, taking his chances. "Would you like to toke up with us before we head home?"

Dumbass stopped in his tracks and looked at Hairy, who was afraid he'd done something to offend the elderly professor.

"I thought you'd never ask," Dumbass said with a giant, shit-eating grin on his face.

Chapter Twelve

"Just don't miss your bus." He added. "I'd hate to have to drive your asses home."

They all laughed.

THE END

Bonus Chapter!!!

British Slang Dictionary

Ace - **awesome**.

Aggro - Short for aggravation

All right? - This is used a lot around London and the south to mean, **"Hello, how are you"**?

Anti-clockwise - **counter-clockwise**

Any road - Up north (where they talk funny!!) instead of saying **anyway**, they say "any road"! Weird huh?

Arse - This is a word that doesn't seem to exist in America. It basically means the same as **ass**, but is much ruder. It is used in phrases like "pain in the arse" (a nuisance) or I "can't be arsed" (I can't be bothered) or you might hear something was "a half arsed attempt" meaning that it was not done properly.

Arse about face - This means you are doing something **back to front**.

Bonus Chapter

Arse over elbow - This is another way of saying **head over heels** but is a little more descriptive.

Arse over tit - Another version of *arse over elbow*, but a bit more graphic!

Arsehole - **Asshole** to you. Not a nice word in either language.

Arseholed - **Drunk**!

As well – Also

Ass - Your backside, but mostly a **donkey**!

Au fait – One of those French expressions that have slipped into the English language. This one means to be **familiar** with something.

Baccy - **Tobacco**. The sort you use to roll your own.

Bang - Nothing to do with your hair - this is a rather unattractive way of describing having **sex**. Always gets a smile from Brits in American hair dressers when they are asked about their bangs.

Barmy - If someone tells you that you're barmy they mean you have gone **mad** or **crazy**.

British Slang Dictionary

Beastly - You would call something or somebody beastly if they were really **nasty** or **unpleasant**.

Bees Knees - This is the polite version of *the dog's bollocks*. So if you are in polite company and want to say that something was **fabulous**, this phrase might come in handy.

Belt up - **shut up**.

Bender - bender doesn't only mean a **gay** man, it also means a **pub crawl** or a **heavy drinking session**.

Bespoke - We say something is bespoke if it has been created especially for someone, in the same way that you say **custom**.

Best of British - **good luck**. It is short for "best of British luck".

Biggie - what a child calls his **poo**! Hence the reason Wendy's Hamburgers has never really taken off in England - who would buy "biggie fries"? Yuck - I'm sure you wouldn't buy **poo fries**! The other meaning of Biggie is **erection**. It just gets worse!

Bite your arm off - someone is over excited to get something.

Bonus Chapter

Bladdered - you are **drunk**.

Blast - An exclamation of surprise.

Blatant - **obvious**.

Bleeding - An alternative to the word *bloody*.

Blimey - Another exclamation of surprise. My Dad used to say "Gawd Blimey" or "Gor Blimey" or even "Cor Blimey". It is all a corruption of the oath **God Blind Me**.

Blinding - If something is a blinding success - it does not mean that any eyes were poked out with sharp sticks - it means it was **awesome**.

Blinkered - Someone who is blinkered is **narrow minded** or narrow sighted - they only see one view on a subject.

Bloody - One of the most useful swear words in English. Mostly used as an exclamation of surprise i.e. "bloody hell" or "bloody nora". Something may be "bloody marvellous" or "bloody awful". It is also used to emphasise almost anything, "you're bloody mad", "not bloody likely" and can also be used in the middle of other words to emphasise them. E.g. "Abso-bloody-lutely"! Americans should avoid saying "bloody" as they sound silly.

British Slang Dictionary

Blooming - Another alternative to the word *bloody*.

Blow me - When an English colleague of mine exclaimed "Blow Me" in front of a large American audience, he brought the house down. It is simply an exclamation of surprise, short for "Blow me down", meaning something like I am so surprised you could knock me over just by blowing. Similar to "Well knock me down with a feather". It is not a request for services to be performed.

Blow off - Who blew off? Means who **farted**?

Blunt - dull.

Bob's your uncle - This is a well used phrase. It is added to the end of sentences a bit like **and that's it!**

Bodge - To do a bodge job means to do a quick and dirty. Make it look good for the next day or two and if it falls down after that - hey well we only bodged it!

Bogey - Booger. Any variety, *crusty dragons* included!

Bollocks - Technically speaking it means **testicles** but is typically used to describe something that is no good (that's bollocks) or that someone is talking

Bonus Chapter

rubbish (he's talking bollocks).

Bomb - really **expensive**.

Bonk - Same meaning as *shag*. Means to **have sex**.

Botch - There are two expressions here - to botch something up or to do a botch job. They both mean that the work done was not of a high standard or was a clumsy patch.

Bottle - This means **courage**. If you have a lotta bottle you have **no fear**.

Box your ears -. Generally meant a **slap** around the head for misbehaving.

Brassed off - you are **fed up**. **Pissed** perhaps.

Brill - Short for "brilliant". Used by kids to mean **cool**.

Budge up - If you want to sit down and someone is taking up too much space, you'd ask them to budge up - **move** and make some space.

Bugger - Like *bloody* it has many uses apart from the obvious dictionary one pertaining to rather unusual sexual habits. The fuller version of this would be "bugger it". It can also be used to tell someone to get lost (bugger off), or to admit defeat (we're buggered) or if you were tired or exhausted you would be buggered. You can also call someone a bugger. When I won £10 on the lottery my mate called me a "lucky bugger".

Bugger all - If something costs bugger all, it means that it costs **nothing**. If you have bugger all, it means you have **nothing**.

Bum - This is the part of your body you sit on. Your **ass**! It might also be someone who is down and out, like a *tramp*.

Bung - To bung something means to **throw** it. A bung is also a **bribe**.

Butchers - To have a butchers at something is to **have a look**.

C of E - The Church of England. Our official **protestant** church - of which the Queen is the head.

Chat up - To chat someone up is to try and **pick them up**.

Cheeky - "Eee you cheeky monkey" was what my mother said to me all the time when I was a kid. Cheeky means you are **flippant**, have too much lip or are a bit of a *smart arse*!

Bonus Chapter

Cheerio - Not a breakfast cereal. Just a friendly way of saying **goodbye**.

Cheers - This word is obviously used when drinking with friends. However, it also has other colloquial meanings. For example when saying **goodbye** you could say "cheers", or "cheers then". It also means **thank you**.

Cheesed off - This is a polite way of saying you are **pissed off** with something.

Chin Wag - This is another word for a **Chat**. You can probably tell why!

Chinese Whispers - This a good one. It refers to the way a story gets changed as is passes from one person to the next so that the end result may be completely different from what was originally said. Sound familiar?

Chivvy along - hurry up!

Chuffed - You would be chuffed to bits if you were really **pleased** about something.

Clear off! - It basically means **get lost**.

Cobblers It means you are talking out of your butt and has nothing to do with any kind of dessert!

British Slang Dictionary

Cock up - A cock up means you have made a **mistake**. It has nothing to do with parts of the male body.

Cockney rhyming slang - There are lots of words that make up cockney rhyming slang. These are basically rhyming words like "butchers hook" which means "look". If you are in London and you hear someone talk about a Septic they are probably talking about you - because it's short for "Septic tank" which equals "yank", which is our word for an American. How do you like that!

Codswallop - My Dad would tell me I was talking a load of codswallop. American kids might be talking **baloney** under the same circumstances.

Cor - You'll often hear a Brit say "cor"! It is another one of those expressions of surprise that we seem to have so many of. ".

Cracking - If something is cracking, it means it is the **best**. Usually said without pronouncing the last "G". If a girl is cracking it means she is **stunning**.

Cram - to **study hard** in the period running up to the exam.

Crap - The same word in both countries - but less rude here.

Bonus Chapter

Crikey - Another exclamation of surprise. Some people say "Crikey Moses".

Crusty dragon - A **booger**. One of the really crispy ones.

Daft - It basically means **stupid**.

Dekko - To have a **look** at something.

Dear - If something is dear it means it is **expensive**. I thought Texan insurance was dear.

Dicky - Dicky rhymes with sicky and means you feel **sick**.

Diddle - To **rip someone off** or to **con** someone is to diddle them.

Dim - A dim person is **stupid** or *thick* or a *dimwit*.

Dimwit - Someone a bit on the dim side.

Dishy - If someone is a bit of a dish or a bit dishy it means they are **attractive** or **good looking**.

DIY - This is short for **do it yourself**

Do - A **party**. You would go to a do if you were going to a party in the UK.

British Slang Dictionary

Do - If you go into a shop and say "do you do batteries?" it means "do you **sell** batteries".

Doddle - Something that is a doddle is a **cinch**, it's easy.

Dodgy - If someone or something is a bit dodgy, it is not to be trusted.

Dog's bollocks - You would say that something **really fantastic** was the dog's bollocks.

Dog's dinner - If you make a real **mess** of something it might be described as a real dog's dinner.

Donkey's years - It means you hadn't seen someone for **ages**.

Drop a clanger – Put your foot in your mouth.

Duck – Dear or love.

Duff - Anything that is duff is **useless, junk, trash**.

Duffer - Any person that is duff could be referred to as a duffer. The Prime Minister was a duffer.

Dull - boring.

Bonus Chapter

Easy Peasy - A childish term for something very easy. You might say it's a **snap**.

Engaged - **busy** signal or the line is **busy**.

Excuse me - This is a great one! It's what kids are taught to say when they belch in public. We are also taught to say "pardon me" if we fart out loud. Unfortunately in American "excuse me" means you are encroaching in someone's personal space and you say "pardon me" when you don't hear someone properly. Imagine our surprise when we discovered that actually Americans are not belching and farting all the time.

Faff - To faff is to **dither** or to *fanny around*.
Fagged - If you are too lazy or tired to do something you could say "I can't be fagged". It means you can't be **Bothered**.

Fagging - Fagging is the practice of making new boys at boarding schools into slaves for the older boys. If you are fagging for an older boy you might find yourself running his bath, cleaning his shoes or performing more undesirable tasks.

Fancy - If you fancy something then it means you **desire** it. Food or a person.

Fanny - This is the word for a woman's **front bits**!

British Slang Dictionary

Fanny around -. It means to **procrastinate**.

Fiddle sticks – Substitute for a swear word.

Filch - To filch is to **steal** or **pilfer**.

Fit -. A fit *bird* means a girl who is pretty **good looking** or tasty! A fit *bloke* would be the male equivalent.

Flog - To Flog something is to **sell** it. Or to beat something or someone with a whip.

Fluke - If something great happened to you by **chance** that would be a fluke.

Flutter - It means to have a **bet**, usually a small one.

Fortnight - **Two weeks**. Comes from an abbreviation of "fourteen nights".

Fruity - If someone is feeling fruity then they are feeling **frisky**.

Full monty - It just means the **whole thing** or going the **whole way**.

Full of beans - This means to have **loads of energy**.

Bonus Chapter

Gagging - Desperate, in a fat slaggy kind of a way.

Gallivanting - It means **fooling around** or **horseplay**.

Gander - It means to **look around**.

Gen - Gen means **information**.

Gen up - To **research a subject** or to **get some information**.

Get lost! - **go away**

Get stuffed! - Even politer way to tell someone to *get lost..*

Getting off - means **making out** or *snogging*.

Give us a bell - This simply means **call me**.

Gobsmacked - Amazed.

Good value - something is a **good deal**.

Goolies – Balls.

Gormless - clueless.

Grem - to spit something out. e.g.

British Slang Dictionary

Grub - **Food**. Similar to *nosh*.

Gutted - **really upset** by something

Haggle - To haggle is to argue or negotiate over a price.

Hanky panky - **making out**

Hard - it means he is ready to fight anything or anybody or to take on any bet after a lot of alcohol.

Hard lines - **bad luck**

Hash - **pound sign** Before you ask, yes it is also something you smoke - see *wacky backy*. Also to make a real hash of something means you really **screwed it up**.

Her Majesty's pleasure - This means being **put in prison** with no release date!

Hiya - Short for **hi there**, this is a friendly way of saying **hello**.

Honking - Honking is **being sick** or **throwing up**.

Horses for courses - This is a common saying that means **each to his own**.

Bonus Chapter

How's your father? - This is a very old term for **sex** which plays on our apparent British sensitivity.

Hump - If you have got the hump it means you are in a **mood**. If you are having a hump, it means you are **having sex**.

Hunky-dory - everything is **cool** and groovy,.

I'm easy - This expression means **I don't care** or **it's all the same to me**.

Jammy - If you are really lucky or **flukey**, you are also very jammy.

John Thomas - Yet another word for a blokes *willy*!

Jolly - it means **very**. So "jolly good" would mean **very good**.

Keep your pecker up - This is one way of saying **keep your chin up**.

Khazi - Another word for the *toilet*. Our version of your **bathroom**.

Kip - A short **sleep**, forty winks, or a snooze.

Knackered - Basically worn out, good for nothing, **tired out**, knackered.

British Slang Dictionary

Knees up - If you're having a knees up, you're going to a **dance** or **party**.

Knob - Yet another word for your *willy*.

Knock off - To knock something off is to **steal** it, not to copy it!

Knock up - This means to **wake someone up**.. Another meaning of this phrase, that is more common these days, is to **make something** out of odds and ends.

Knockers - Another word for **breasts**.

Knuckle sandwich - **thump you in the face**.

Leg it - This is a way of saying **run** or **run for it**.

Left, right and centre - searching **all over**.

Love bite - You call them **hickies** - the things you do to yourself as a youngster with the vacuum cleaner attachment to make it look like someone *fancies* you!

Lurgy - you are **ill**, you have the **Flu**.

Luvvly-jubbly - Clearly another way of saying **lovely**.

Bonus Chapter

Mate - Most chaps like to go to the pub with their mates. Mate means **friend** or *chum*. .

Mufti - An old army term for your "civvies". Civilian clothes that is, rather than your uniform.

Mug - If someone is a bit of a mug, it means they are **gullible**.

Mush - Slang word for your mouth as in "shut your mush".

Mutt's nuts - If something is described as being "the Mutt's" then you'll know it is **fantastic** or **excellent**. "The Mutt's" is short for "The Mutt's nuts" which is clearly another way of saying the *"Dog's Bollocks"*! All clear now?

Naff - If something is naff, it is basically **uncool**.

Nancy boy - If someone is being pathetic you would call them a nancy or a nancy boy. It's also another word for a **gay** man.

Nark - If someone is in a nark, it means they are in a **bad mood**, or being grumpy. It's also the word for a **spy** or **informant**.

Narked - In the UK you would say that someone looked narked if you thought they were in a bad mood.

British Slang Dictionary

Nesh - **pathetic** or a bit of a *nancy boy*.

Nice one! - **good job**

Nick - To nick is to **steal**.

Nicked - Something that has been **stolen** has been nicked.

Nitwit - See *twit*.

Nookie - Nookie is the same as *hanky panky*. Something you do with your *bird*!

Nosh - **Food**.

Not my cup of tea - This is a common saying that means something is **not to your liking**.

Nowt - This is Yorkshire for **nothing**. Similarly *owt* is Yorkshire for **anything**.

Nut - To nut someone is to **head butt** them.

Off colour - If someone said you were off colour they would mean that you look **pale** and **ill**!

Off your trolley - raving bonkers, **crazy**, **mad**!

On about - It means what are you **talking about**?

Bonus Chapter

On the job - If you are on the job, it could mean that you are **hard at work**, or **having sex**. Usually the context helps you decide which it is!

On the piss - out to **get drunk**, or to get *pissed*.

On your bike - A very polite way of telling someone to f*** off.

One off - A one off is a **special** or a **one time** event that is never to be repeated. Like writing this book!

Owt - This is Yorkshire for **anything**. Similarly *nowt* is Yorkshire for **nothing**.

Pants - something which is **total crap** is "pants".

Pardon me - This is very amusing for Brits in America. Most kids are taught to say "pardon me" if they fart in public or at the table etc. In America it has other meanings which take us Brits a while to figure out. I thought I was surrounded by people with flatulence problems!

Parky - a word to describe the weather as being **rather cold**!

Pass - This means **I don't know**

British Slang Dictionary

Pavement pizza - a descriptive way of saying **vomit**.

Peanuts - means something is **cheap**.

Pear shaped - If something has gone pear shaped it means it has become a **disaster**..

Piece of cake - It means **it's a cinch**!

Pinch - This means to **steal** something, more like taking something from your own kitchen though.

Pip pip - Another out-dated expression meaning **goodbye**.

Piss poor - If something is described as being "piss poor" it means it is an **extremely poor** attempt at something.

Piss up - A piss up is a **drinking session**.

Pissed - means getting **drunk**.

Pissing around - **Fooling about**..

Plastered - Another word for **loaded**, drunk

Porkies - **lies**.

Bonus Chapter

Porridge - Doing porridge means to **serve time** in prison.

Posh - Roughly translates as **high class**,

Potty - means you are a little **crazy**,

Prat - Yet another mildly insulting name for someone.

PTO - This is an abbreviation for "please turn over". You will see it on forms in the UK where you would see the single word **over** in the USA.

Puff - another word for a **fart**.

Pukka - means **super** or **smashing**.

Pull - means **looking for woman or a man at a pub.**

Pussy - This is what we call our **cat**,

Put a sock in it - This is one way of telling someone to **shut up**.

Put paid to - This is an expression which means **to put an end to something**.

British Slang Dictionary

Queer - Apart from the obvious gay link, this word used to be used a lot to mean someone looked **ill**.

Quid - A **pound** in money is called a quid. It is the equivalent to the **buck** or **clam** in America. A five pound note is called a fiver and a ten pound note is called a tenner.

Quite - When used alone, this word means the same as **absolutely**!

Rat arsed - Yet another term for **drunk**, *sloshed* or *plastered*.

Read - If someone asks you what you read at *university*, they mean what was your **major** at school.

Redundancy - If you are made redundant it means you are **laid off**.

Reverse the charges - call collect.

Right - I'm feeling right *knackered*. That would mean you were feeling **very** tired.

Ring - You would ring someone on the phone not **call** them, in the UK.

Bonus Chapter

Roger - My Oxford English Dictionary says **to copulate**. You might say **screw**.

Round - When you hear the words "your round" in the pub, it means it is your turn to **buy the drinks** for everyone in the group.

Row - Rhymes with "cow" this means an **argument**.

Rubbish - The stuff we put in the *bin*. **Trash** or **garbage** to you.

Rugger - This is short for "rugby". It is a contact sport similar to your **football** but played in muddy fields during winter and rain. Not only that, but the players wear almost no protection!

Rumpy pumpy - Another word for *hanky panky*, or a bit of *nookie*!

Sack/sacked - If someone gets the sack it means they are **fired**.

Sad - This is a common word, with the same meaning as *naff*. Used in expressions like "you sad b***ard".

Scrummy - This is a word that would be used to describe either some food that was particularly good (and probably sweet and fattening).

British Slang Dictionary

Scrumping - To go **stealing** - usually apples from someone else's trees!

Send-up - To send someone up is to **make fun** of them.

Shag - Same as *bonk* but slightly less polite.

Shagged - Past tense of *shag*, but also see *knackered*.

Shambles - If something is a shambles it is **chaotic** or a real **mess**.

Shambolic - In a state of **chaos**.

Shirty - It means **bad tempered**.

Shite - This is just another way of saying **shit**.

Shitfaced - If you hear someone saying that they got totally shitfaced it means they were out on the town and got steaming **drunk**.

Shufti - Pronounced shooftee, this means to take a **look** at something.

Sixes and sevens - If something is all at sixes and sevens then it is in a mess, topsy turvy or somewhat haywire!

Bonus Chapter

Skew-whiff - This is what you would call **crooked**.

Skive - To skive is to **evade** something.

Slag - To slag someone off, is to **bad mouth** them in a nasty way. Usually to their face.

Slapper - A slapper is a female who is a bit loose. A bit like a *slag* or a *tart*. Probably also translates into **tramp** in American.

Slash - Something a *lager lout* might be seen doing in the street after his curry - having a slash. Other expressions used to describe this bodily function include; siphon the python, shake the snake, wee, **pee**, piss, piddle and having a *jimmy*.

Sloshed - Yet another way to describe being **drunk**.

Smarmy - Another word for a **smoothy**, someone who has a way with the ladies for example.

Smart - When *we* say someone is smart, we are talking about the way they are dressed - you might say they look **sharp**.

Smashing - If something is smashing, it means it is **terrific**.

British Slang Dictionary

Smeg - This is a rather disgusting word, popularised by the TV show, Red Dwarf. Short for smegma, the dictionary definition says it is a "sebaceous secretion from under the foreskin". Now you know why it has taken me 3 years to add it in here. Not nice! Rather worryingly smeg is also the name of a company that makes ovens!!!

Snap - This is the name of a card game where the players turn cards at the same time and shout "snap" when they match. People also say "snap" when something someone else says has happened to them too. For example when I told somebody that my *wallet* was stolen on holiday, they said "snap", meaning that theirs had too!

Snog - If you are out on the *pull* you will know you are succeeding if you end up snogging someone of the opposite sex (or same sex for that matter!). It would probably be referred to as **making out** in American, or serious kissing!

Snookered - If you are snookered it means you are up the famous creek without a paddle. It comes from the game of snooker where you are unable to hit the ball because the shot is blocked by your opponent's ball.

Sod - This word has many uses. My father always used to say "Oh Sod!" or "Sod it!" if something went wrong and he didn't want to swear too badly in front of the children. If someone is a sod or an "old sod" then it means they are a bit of a **bastard** or an old *git*. "Sod off" is like saying "piss off" or "get lost" & "sod you" means something like "f*** off". It also means a chunk of lawn of course. You can usually tell the difference!

Sod all - **nothing**.

Sod's law - **Murphy's law** - whatever can go wrong, will go wrong.

Sorted - When you have **fixed a problem**

Speciality - This is another one where you chaps drop your "I". when I first saw **specialty** written down in the US I thought it was a mistake. But no! We love our I's!

Splash out - If you splash out on something - it means you throw your senses out the window, get out your credit card and **spend far too much money**.

Squidgy - A chocolate cream cake would be squidgey. It means to be **soft** and, well, squidgey!

Squiffy - This means you are feeling a little **drunk**.

Starkers - means **stark naked**.

British Slang Dictionary

Stiffy - Yet another word for **erection**.

Stone the crows - This is an old expression with the same meaning as "cor *blimey*".

Stonker - This means something is huge. It is also used to refer to an **erection**! Clearly English modesty is a myth!

Stonking - This weird word means **huge**.

Strop - If someone is **sulking** or being particularly miserable you would say they are being stroppy or that they have a strop on.

Stuff - polite way of saying f*** it. Who cares! Stuff it! You can also say "stuff him" or "stuff her" meaning they can *sod off*.

Suss – figure it out.

Sweet fanny adams - This means **nothing** or *sod all*.

Swotting - Swotting means to **study hard**, the same as *cram* does.

Ta - short for **thanks**.

Taking the biscuit - **out-does** everything else and cannot be bettered.

Bonus Chapter

Taking the mickey - See *taking the piss*. Variations include "taking the mick" and "taking the Michael".

Taking the piss - means **making fun** of someone.

Talent - Talent is the same as *totty*. Checking out the talent means looking for the sexy young girls (or boys I suppose).

Tara - Pronounced "churar", this is another word for *cheerio* or **goodbye**.

Throw a spanner in the works - **to wreck something**.

Tickety-boo - something is **going well**

Tidy - Apart from the obvious meaning of **neat**, tidy also means that a woman is a looker, **attractive** or sexy.

Todger - As if we don't have enough of them already, this is yet another word for your *willy*, or **penis**.

Toodle pip - This is an old expression meaning **goodbye**.

Tool - Yet another word for your *willy* or **penis**.

British Slang Dictionary

Tosser - This is another word for *wanker* and has exactly the same meaning and shares the same hand signal.

Totty - If a chap is out looking for totty, he is looking for a nice **girl** to chat up.

TTFN - Short for "ta ta for now". Which in turn means **goodbye**!

Twat - Another word used to insult someone who has upset you. Also means the same as *fanny* but is less acceptable in front of your grandmother, as this refers to parts of the female anatomy. Another use for the same word is to twat something, which would be to **hit** it hard. Get it right or I'll twat you over the head!

Twee - It means **dainty** or **quaint**.

Twit - You twit! Not so rude as calling someone an **idiot** but it amounts to the same thing.

Two finger salute - When you see a Brit stick up two fingers at you in a V shape, he may be ordering two of something (if his palms are toward you). The other way around and it's an insult along the lines of your one finger salute.

Bonus Chapter

Uni - Short for university, we would say we went to uni like you would say you went to **school**. School here is just for kids.

Wacky backy - This is the stuff in a joint, otherwise known as **pot** or **marijuana**!

Waffle - To waffle means to **talk** on and on about nothing.

Wangle - Some people have all the luck. I know some people that can wangle anything; upgrades on planes, better rooms in hotels. You know what I mean.

Wank - This is the verb to describe the action a *wanker* participates in.

Wanker - This is a derogatory term used to describe someone who is a bit of a **jerk**. It actually means someone who masturbates and also has a hand signal that can be done with one hand at people that cannot see you shouting "wanker" at them. This is particularly useful when driving.

Watcha - Simply means **Hi**. Also short for "what do you" as in "watcha think of that"?

Waz - It means **wee** or **pee**.

British Slang Dictionary

Welly - If you "give it welly", it means you are **trying harder** or **giving it the boot**. Welly is also short for *wellington boots*, which are like your **galoshes**.

Whinge - Whingers are not popular in any circumstance. To whinge is to **whine**.

Willy - Another word for **penis** for polite company.

Wind up - This has a couple of meanings. If something you do is a "wind up" it means you are **making fun** of someone. However it you are "wound up" it means you are **annoyed**.

Wobbler - To "throw a wobbly" or to "throw a wobbler" means to **have a tantrum**.

Wonky - If something is **shaky** or **unstable** you might say it is wonky.

Yakking - This means **talking incessantly** - not that I know anyone who does that now!

Yonks - "Blimey, I haven't heard from you for yonks". If you heard someone say that it would mean that they had not seen you for **ages**!

Bonus Chapter

Zed - The last letter of the alphabet. The English hate saying **zee** and only relent with names such as ZZ Top (Zed Zed Top does sound a bit stupid!).

Zonked - If someone is zonked or "zonked out" it means they are totally *knackered* or you might say **exhausted**.

NOW AVAILABLE!!!

Poop Happens!" in this send up of all things cowboy!

So, Who Was That Masked Guy Anyway? is the story of Ernie, the grandson of the original Masked Cowboy, a lawman who fought for truth, justice and the cowboy way in the old west. Now that Grandpa is getting on in years he's looking for someone to carry on for him. The only problem? Ernie doesn't know anything about being a cowboy. He's never seen a real cow, he's allergic to milk and to tell the truth he doesn't know one end of a horse from another! So it's off to cowboy school to learn the basics of cowboyology. He'll learn to rope and ride, chew and spit and to develop the perfect "Yee-Haw!". And it's a good thing, because a band of no good outlaws have captured the good people of Gabby Gulch and the President of the United States, Theodore Roosevelt! Now it's up to Ernie and his friends to save the day...but beware, before it's all over, the poop is sure to hit the fans!

NOW AVAILABLE!!!

WANTED: SANTA CLAUS is the story of what happens when
a group of department store moguls led by the greedy B. G.
Bucks decide to replace Santa Claus with the shiny new
"KRINGLE 3000", codenamed...ROBO-SANTA! A new Father
Christmas with a titanium alloy outer shell housing a nuclear
powered drive train, not to mention a snow white beard and a
jolly disposition! These greedy tycoons will stop at nothing to
get rid of jolly old St. Nick. That includes framing him for such
crimes as purse snatching, tire theft and...oh no...not.....puppy
kicking??!! Say it isn't so Santa! Now it's up to Santa's elves to
save the day! But Santa's in no shape to take on his stainless
steel counterpart! He'll have to train for his big comeback.
Enter Mickey, one of the toughest elves of all time! He'll get
Santa ready for the big showdown! But it's going to mean
reaching deep down inside to find "the eye of the reindeer"!

NOW AVAILABLE!!!

At the edge of the universe sits The Long John Cafe. A place where the average guy and the average "Super" guy can sit and have a cup of coffee and just be themselves...or, someone else if that's what they want. The cafe is populated by iconic figures of the 20th Century, including cowboys, hippies, super heroes and movie stars. They've come to celebrate the end of the old Century and the beginning of tomorrow! That is, if they make it through the night! It seems the evil Dr. McNastiman has other plans for our heroes. Like their total destruction!

NOW AVAILABLE!!!

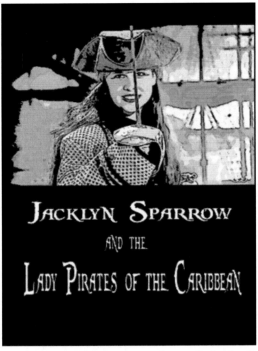

Why should the boys get to have all the fun?

Jacklyn Sparrow and the Lady Pirates of the Caribbean is our brand new swashbuckling pirate parody complete with bloodthirsty buccaneers in massive sword clanking battle scenes!! A giant wise cracking parrot named Polly!! Crazy obsessions with eye liner!! And just who is Robert, the Dreaded Phylum Porifera??

Of course the whole thing ends with a large celebration where everybody gets down with their bad selves!! It's fun for the whole family in this lampoon of everything you love about pirates!!!

NOW AVAILABLE!!!

"May the Dwarf be with you!"

A wacky take on the classic fairy tale which will have audiences rolling in the floor with laughter!

What happens when you mix an articulate mirror, a conceited queen, a prince dressed in purple, seven little people with personality issues, a basket of kumquats and a little Star Wars for good measure?

Snow White and the Seven Dwarves of the Old Republic!

NOW AVAILABLE!!!

An ode to the potty.

"My dreams of thee flow softly.
They enter with tender rush.
The still soft sound which echoes,
When I lower the lid and flush."

They say that porcelain is the best antenna for creativity. At least that's
what this cast of young people believe in Dear John: An ode to the
potty! The action of this one act play takes place almost entirely behind
the doors of five bathroom stalls. This short comedy is dedicated to all
those term papers, funny pages and Charles Dickens' novels that have
been read behind closed (stall) doors!

Bathroom humor at its finest!

NOW AVAILABLE!!!

ELVIS MEETS NIXON
(OPERATION WIGGLE)

Declassified after 40 years!

On December 21, 1970, an impromptu meeting took place between the King of Rock and Roll and the Leader of the Free World.

Elvis Meets Nixon (Operation Wiggle) is a short comedy which offers one possible (and ultimately ridiculous) explanation of what happened during that meeting.

NOW AVAILABLE!!!

𝔈𝔳𝔢𝔫 𝔄𝔡𝔞𝔪

**In the beginning, there was a man.
Then there was a woman.
And then there was this piece of fruit...
...and that's when everything went horribly wrong!
Even Adam is a short comedy exploring the relationship
between men and women right from day one.**

**Why doesn't he ever bring her flowers like he used to?
Why doesn't she laugh at his jokes anymore?
And just who is that guy in the red suit?
And how did she convince him to eat that fruit, anyway?**

NOW AVAILABLE!!!

Count Dracula is bored. He's pretty much sucked Transylvania dry, and he's looking for a new challenge. So it's off to New York, New York! The Big Apple! The town that never sleeps...that'll pose a challenge for sure.
Dracula purchases The Carfax Theatre and decides to put on a big, flashy Broadway show...

THE DRACULA SPECTACULA!

Of course the Theatre just happens to be across the street from Dr. Seward's Mental Hospital where people have been mysteriously dying since The Count moved in.
Just a coincidence?
The play features a large cast of zany characters and is equal parts horror story and Broadway show spoof!

NOW AVAILABLE!!!

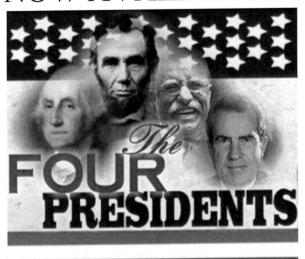

The FOUR PRESIDENTS

THE FOUR PRESIDENTS examines the lives and characters of four of the most colorful personalities to hold the office. Much of the dialogue comes from the Presidents' own words.

THE FARMER WHO WOULD BE KING presents George Washington through his own words, and the words of his biographer Mason Locke Weems. Was the father of our country a simple farmer who answered the call of his countrymen, or something more?

THE GREAT EMANCIPATOR is the story of a simple man. Born in the wilds of Kentucky and mostly self taught, Abraham Lincoln would someday be regarded as the greatest American who ever lived.

THE BULL MOOSE who occupied the White House 100 years ago was truly a man of action. Theodore Roosevelt was a father, author, rancher, sportsman, policeman, Rough Rider, cowboy, big game hunter, Governor of New York and eventually The President of the United States!

NIXON AND THE GHOSTS is a surreal drama with dialogue ripped straight from the headlines. On the night before his resignation, Nixon ponders his rise and fall, as the shadows themselves seem to come alive and he is confronted by the spirits of Presidents past!

NOW AVAILABLE!!!

The lights rise on a beautiful sunset.
A mermaid is silhouetted against an ocean backdrop.
Hauntingly familiar music fills the air.
Then...the Lawyer shows up.
And that's when the fun really begins!
The Little Mermaid (More or Less.) is the story of a Theatre
company attempting to stage a children's version of the Hans
Christian Anderson classic. The only problem? It looks and
sounds an awful lot like a movie of the same name. That's when
the Lawyer for a certain "mouse eared company" starts talking
lawsuit for copyright infringement.
Lawsuit?
Copyright infringement?
Throw out the costumes!
What's that? There's a bunch of old clothes backstage from the
1970's? Well, don't just stand there! Go get them!
Ditch the music!
What? Somebody's mom has a greatest disco hits cd out in the
car? That'll be perfect!
Change everyone's names!
Tartar Sauce! Little M.! The Crab Formerly Known as Sebastian!
Everybody ready? Ok...Action!!!

NOW AVAILABLE!!!

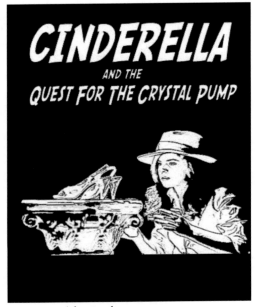

Adventure has a new name...

CINDERELLA!!!

Cinderella and the Quest for the Crystal Pump, is the story of a young girl seeking a life beyond the endless chores heaped upon her by her grouchy stepmother and two stepsisters.

Mow the grass! Beat the rugs! Churn the buttermilk!

Sometimes it's more than one girl can take!
More than anything, Cinderella wants to go to the prince's masquerade ball, but there's one problem...she has nothing to wear! Luckily, her Fairy Godperson has a few ideas.

Meanwhile, Prince Charles Edward Tiberius Charming III, or "Charlie" as he prefers to be called, has run away with his pals, Touchstone the Jester and the Magic Mirror, searching for a quiet place where he can just enjoy a good book!

Now this mismatched quartet find themselves on a quest to find the greatest treasure of all...the perfect pair of Crystal Pumps!

NOW AVAILABLE!!!

Shorespeare is loosely based on a Midsummer Night's Dream. Shakespeare, with the help of Cupid, has landed at the Jersey Shore. Cupid inspires him to write a play about two New Jersey sweethearts, Cleo and Toni. Shakespeare is put off by their accent and way of talking, but decides to send the two teenagers on a course of true love. Toni and Cleo are determined to get married right after they graduate from high school, but in order to do so they must pass this course of true love that Cupid's pixies create and manipulate. As they travel along the boardwalk at the Jersey Shore, Cleo and Toni, meet a handful of historical figures disguised as the carnies. Confucius teaches Cleo the "Zen of Snoring", Charles Ponzi teaches them the importance of "White Lies", Leonardo Da Vinci shows them the "Art of Multitasking", and finally they meet Napolean who tries to help them to "Accept Shortcomings" of each other. After going through all these lessons, the sweethearts decide that marriage should wait, and Cupid is proud of Shakespeare who has finally reached out to the modern youth.

NOW AVAILABLE!!!

Everyone has heard the phrase, "it's the squeaky wheel that gets the oil," but how many people know the Back-story? The story begins in a kingdom far, far away over the rainbow – a kingdom called Spokend. This kingdom of wheels is a happy one for the gods have blessed the tiny hamlet with plentiful sunshine, water and most important –oil. Until a terrible drought starts to dry up all the oil supplies. What is to be done?

The powerful barons of industry and politicians decide to hold a meeting to decide how to solve the situation. Since Spokend is a democracy all the citizens come to the meeting but their voices are ignored – especially the voice of one of the poorer citizens of the community suffering from a squeak that can only be cured with oil, Spare Wheel and his wife Fifth Wheel. Despite Spare Wheel's desperate pleas for oil, he is ignored and sent home without any help or consideration.

Without oil, Spare Wheel's squeak becomes so bad he loses his job and his family starts to suffer when his sick leave and unemployment benefits run out. What is he to do? Spare Wheel and Fifth Wheel develop a scheme that uses the squeak to their advantage against the town magistrate Big Wheel who finally relents and gives over the oil. Thus, for years after in the town of Spokend citizens in need of help are told "It's the squeaky wheel that gets the oil."

Made in United States
North Haven, CT
18 January 2022

14935526R00093